ANCIENT
ECHOES

ANCIENT ECHOES

Refusing the Fear-Filled,
Greed-Driven Toxicity of
the Far Right

WALTER BRUEGGEMANN

Fortress Press
Minneapolis

For
Christina McHugh Brueggemann, MD

Contents

Contents

Preface

In his book, Evil *Geniuses: The Unmaking of America: A Recent History* (2020), Kurt Andersen has provided something of a roadmap for the history, ideology, and intent of the right wing as a political force among us. In these several pages, I have responded to Anderson's rich, suggestive work, and have played upon his own articulation of the right wing. I have done so for two reasons. First, I have no doubt that the Bible provides guidance and resources for our current political situation, and standing ground from which to resist current right-wing ideology, and to host alternative visions of social well-being. My title, *Ancient Echoes*, intends to reflect that conviction. The Bible, ancient as it is, continues to emit echoes that take the form of both assurance and summons. The assurance from biblical faith, variously expressed, is that there is a coherent governance of creation that is bent toward well-being, shaped as restorative justice, and enacted with generous compassion. The summons that echoes from the Bible, also variously voiced, is that we human agents are recruited into that work of well-being, in the shaping of social practices, policies, and institutions toward justice, and into the daily practice of generous compassion. These echoes (which are readily available, as we have ears to hear) offer firm standing ground that is contrasted with the fearful, greedy, hated-filled intent of the Far Right that tilts too readily toward violence. It is possible to "stand on the promises!"

Second, and of equal importance and with urgent practicality, I believe that the communities directly funded by the biblical tradition, the synagogue and the church, are indeed summoned and authorized to speak out on the force of right-wing ideology on behalf of hospitable neighborliness. It is now high time for the synagogues and their rabbis, and the churches and their pastors, to speak out about this crisis moment in our society. These communities have a deep stake in the flourishing of democracy, and a solid reason for refusing and resisting the propensity of fascism that wants to reduce political influence to the privileged and entitled few.

These expositions are my modest attempt to exhibit the ways in which biblical faith offers a compelling alternative to the politics of fear and violence. In each instance, I have juxtaposed a right-wing claim—as delineated by Andersen—with a biblical text. That juxtaposition, in each case, I take to be persuasive. But I could have as well appealed to other texts, precisely because the Bible teems with testimony to a different sort of public practice that is in sync with the will and intent of the good, generous creator God.

It is my hope and intent that this little collection might be of some use in these communities of faith. I hope that it might be a resource for congregational leaders (rabbis and pastors) who are ready to step up to the hard, demanding public issues. And perhaps this collection might be a useful resource for congregational study. I have no doubt that if there is to be a sustained resistance to the current turn among us from greed through fear to violence, it will be based in such communities that have staying power, courageous leadership, and that are deeply and knowingly grounded in the biblical text.

I finish with these waves of deep gratitude:

- First to Mary Brown. I first wrote these pieces for her blog platform, churchanew.org. I am grateful for her permit and encouragement with them, and now to circulate them more widely.
- Second, I am abidingly grateful to Carey Newman and his Fortress Press colleagues, for their willingness and readiness to move these pages along to publication.
- Third, and most important, I am grateful to Tia Brueggemann, who is *sine qua non* for my work. Not only does she edit my work in ways that protect me from too much carelessness but she is my continuing interlocutor on these urgent issues.

On all counts I am grateful to be able to continue my work into old age, and grateful for the good company of readers who lend me their support and encouragement.

I am glad to salute Christina McHugh Brueggemann who continues to practice her fine medical arts with a caring human face.

Walter Brueggemann
Columbia Theological Seminary

1

The Possibility of Good Governance

In his remarkable, important book, *Evil Geniuses: The Unmaking of America: A Recent History* (2020), Kurt Andersen has traced the long-term, quite cynical, and ruthless planning of the Right to take over the government. (The takeover of the Supreme Court by the Right happened after Andersen's book was written, but it fits the plan and the pattern.) Near the end of his book, Andersen lists eight claims in the playbook of the Right that generate their action and feed the uncritical public that has a right-wing appetite. It is my intention in this and following chapters to take up each of these eight distortions of political reality, and to consider how we may in good faith respond to them. I have no doubt that a careful pointed response to each of these distortions is an effort worth making. I will take up each claim in turn.

The first claim is·that **government is bad**. The proposition is uninflected and without any limit or qualification. It means "all government." Specifically, it means the present government. The claim has no doubt come from those who imagine themselves to be *self-made*, *self-sufficient*, and *self-secure*, and who regard any government action as simply an unwelcome intrusion on their self-made lives. Such a sentiment of course abhors any government regulation that in every case is seen to be an inappropriate check against limitless self-aggrandizement. The claim was given popular articulation by the genial comment of Ronald Reagan, who asserted that the nine most terrifying words are "I'm from the government and I'm here to help." Andersen notes that in this same speech, Reagan also bragged about the billions of federal dollars he had given to farmers, not wanting us to notice that the government did indeed help farmers. Andersen also notes that the same claim was subsequently reiterated by Donald Trump, who also wanted to denigrate the government. But the sweeping claim about the government is posturing, and is not meant to be taken seriously or literally, because many right-wing folk benefit greatly from the government.

In response the work is to make the case that not all government is bad, and that we can (a) distinguish between bad government and good government, and (b) that we may work to assure and effect good government. As a basis for a response to this false claim of the Right, I suggest an appeal to the prophetic declaration of Ezekiel 34:2–24. At the outset, we may recognize that it is a long-standing practice in the Near East (at least as early as Hammurabi) to utilize the metaphor of "shepherd" to refer to ruler. Thus the imagery of "shepherd–sheep" in this chapter of Ezekiel refers to government, specifically the Davidic dynasty in Jerusalem, and the designation of Israel in the imagery as the "sheep" that are cared for by the "shepherd" king.

The first part of the prophetic declaration is a description of the "bad government" in Jerusalem, a long series of Davidic kings who acted in self-serving ways to the detriment of "the sheep":

Thus says the Lord God: Ah, shepherds of Israel
who have been feeding yourselves! Should not
shepherds feed the sheep? You eat the fat, you
clothe yourself with the wool, you slaughter
the fatlings; but you do not feed the sheep. You
have not strengthened the weak, you have not
healed the sick, you have not bound up the
injured, you have not brought back the strayed,
you have not sought the lost, but with force
and harshness you have ruled them. (vv. 2–4)

The statement manages to allude to the duties and
failures of the royal government while still staying
inside the imagery of shepherd–sheep. The shepherds
have been preoccupied with self-serving and self-
indulgence, and so have neglected the proper duties
of governance. The duties include feeding the sheep,
strengthening the weak; healing the sick; bringing
back the strayed, that is, a viable economy with no
one left behind; a good security system; and effective health care delivery. These are the staples of good
government. But the Davidic dynasty has failed in
all of these duties, because it has been self-serving in
greedy ways.

The outcome of such failed, self-indulgent government, says the prophet, is a "scattering" (v. 5), that is, destruction, exile, and displacement. In prophetic rendering it is the greedy failure of government that has resulted in the terminal crisis of displacement in Jerusalem at the hands of the Babylonians. The "wild animals" of verse 8 refers to the marauding forces of Israel's enemies, notably the Assyrians and then Babylonians. Thus, this government is bad!

But it need not be so. Government is not intrinsically bad. Good government is possible when the "shepherds" get their minds off of self-gain and give attention and priority to the well-being of the sheep. Thus, the prophetic declaration moves beyond the condemnation of the failed government of the Davidic regime, and anticipates a new, effective, reliable government that will lead to security, prosperity, and well-being. The prospect for good government is the resolve of YHWH, who declares that "I, myself" will be the shepherd (v. 11). What follows in verses 12–16 is a guideline for what constitutes good government, an inventory that reflects YHWH's own resolve for good government in Israel. This is what a good government will do:

I will seek out my sheep. I will rescue them from all the places to which they have been scattered on a day of clouds and thick darkness. I will bring them out from the peoples and gather them from the countries, and bring them into their own land; and I will feed them on the mountains of Israel, by the watercourses, and in all the inhabited parts of the land. I will feed them with good pasture, and the mountain heights of Israel shall be their pasture. There they shall lie down in good grazing land, and they shall feed on rich pasture on the mountains of Israel. I myself will be the shepherd of my sheep, and I will make them lie down, says the Lord God. I will seek the lost, and I will bring back the strayed, and I will bind up the injured, and I will strengthen the weak, but the fat and strong I will destroy. I will feed them with justice. (vv. 12–16)

The declaration pertains to Israel displaced in exile, so that the work of the shepherd government is to recover and restore the sheep that have been dislocated. The work of good government is restoration, with particular attention to the lost, the injured, and the weak. The work of this government is nothing less than restorative justice for the sheep that have been abused by bad, neglectful government. At the end of this statement, Ezekiel steps outside the imagery of shepherd–sheep to speak of justice, for one cannot speak of *good government* without a passion for *restorative justice*, that is, preoccupation with the requirements of the needy, weak, and poor.

Two other affirmations are made by the prophet at the end of this text. In verses 20–21 the prophetic declaration exhibits an awareness of the crucial social differentiation between the powerful and the vulnerable. In the imagery of "shepherd–sheep," the powerful who exploit and prey upon the vulnerable are seen as "fat sheep" who act in greedy, selfish, aggressive ways to secure more than a fair share of the available food:

> Because you pushed with flank and shoulder,
> and butted at all the weak animals with your
> horns until you scattered them far and wide.
> (v. 21)

The aggressive verbs, "push" and "butt," witness to aggressive socioeconomic action of the most exploitative kind. The "good shepherd" = good government consists not of being a passive umpire but of weighing in effectively and decisively on behalf of the weak and vulnerable. Thus good government sides with the vulnerable, a clear articulation of "God's preferential option for the poor." In order to reset the socioeconomic equation, we may imagine that the shepherd's corrective action takes the form of something like *reparations*, in order that the "weak sheep" might share a fair share of the resources of the community.

Finally, in verses 23–25, the prophet mentions the human king, David, the anticipated heir of the dynasty who will be the "good king," the leader of a restorative regime. Until this point in the chapter, we can see that the new good governance is the work of God. God engages in "direct rule" when human kings have failed and reneged on their leadership responsibility. But lest this oracle lack historical specificity, these final words make clear that the work of good government is the work of human governance. It is human work to exercise good governance. And good governance consists of protection of the weak, the strayed, the lost, and the vulnerable from the predation of the powerful. It is the work of the Davidic king to do the work of restorative justice. The same point is reiterated in the royal Psalm 72:

For he delivers the needy when they call,
the poor and those who have no helper.
He has pity on the weak and the needy,
and saves the lives of the needy.
From oppression and violence he redeems
their life;
and precious is their blood in his sight.
(Psalm 72:12–14)

Christians will read this Davidic reference in Ezekiel toward the governance of Jesus. And indeed, the New Testament attests that Jesus enacted the alternative governance of the Kingdom of God. Jesus engages in restorative action toward the vulnerable who have been the victims of an aggressive regime:

The blind receive their sight, the lame walk,
the lepers are cleansed, the deaf hear, the dead
are raised, the poor have good news brought to
them. (Luke 7:22)

Jesus does the work of the anticipated good Davidic king.

But of course, we read this charter for good government in Ezekiel beyond the direct rule of God, beyond the historic role of the Davidic dynasty, and beyond the specificity of Jesus. We read this charter for good government with our reference to our own political institutions and circumstances. The conclusion toward which this prophetic charter presses is that not all government is bad; good government is possible. Good government requires that those with power and leverage may use their energy toward common well-being that entails restorative action for those "left behind." Bad government, of which we have plenty, occurs when the leverage of government is mobilized for self-advancement and self-gain. It is for good reason that the left behind—including many people of color—hope and work for a strong government that can weigh in on social inequity, and do restorative work for the sake of the lost, the strayed, the injured, and the weak. There is, in like manner, good reason for those with self-serving leverage to want a weak and ineffective government in order to be unencumbered in their capacity to "push and butt" without restraint. Such interests, in the words of Grover Norquist, want a government the "size of a bath tub." The argument about the work and size of government is not a disinterested conversation. It concerns the capacity of a good government that can restrain the forces of exploitative greed. We in the US are now in a most precarious position wherein the pushing, butting, "fat sheep," with sharp horns, control much of the government. That way, as the prophet knows, leads to the "scattering" of the weak and the vulnerable. The insistence of Ezekiel is that such destructive government will fail. We can indeed choose otherwise and insist upon another sort of government that is not predatory. But that will require that "lean sheep" insist upon otherwise. In imagining the alternative, Ezekiel will not call the good expected human ruler a "king," but only a "prince" (v. 24). The real and final king is the Lord of restorative justice, in whose service good government will engage. The church must bear witness to the possibility of good government and guide the sort of discernment that will result in such restorative government.

2

The Discomfiting Gift of Newness

The second right-wing claim listed in Kurt Andersen's *Evil Geniuses* is **belief in our perfect, mythical yesteryear**. This claim by the Right is the wish or hope to escape a present social reality into an imagined past that was found to be more congenial and less demanding. Such an exercise in nostalgia is highly selective about the past, with a capacity to forget or deny the many liabilities of that past for the sake of a pretend world.

In the world of ancient Israel, that act of escapist nostalgia is on exhibit in Psalm 137. While we tend to focus on the hoped-for vengeance voice in the Psalm, we may notice that there is a longing for a remembered Jerusalem that is precious and treasured:

> If I forget you, O Jerusalem,
> let my right hand wither!
> Let my tongue cling to the roof of my mouth,
> if I do not remember you,
> if I do not set Jerusalem above my highest joy.
>   (Psalm 137:5–6)

That remembered Jerusalem, however, is very different from the city characterized in prophetic poetry or, for that matter, in the narrative account of the kings. The prophetic lines castigate those who are "at ease in Zion" who engage in self-indulgence (6:1):

> Alas for those who lie on beds of ivory, and
>   lounge on their couches,
> and eat lambs from the flock,
> and calves from the stall;
> who sing idle songs to the sound of the harp,
> and like David improvise on instruments of
>   music;
> who drink wine from bowls,

and anoint themselves with the finest oils.
(Amos 6:4–6)

Those who engage in such luxury, however, failed to notice the profound crisis into which the city had entered; so narcoticized, they were "not grieved over the ruin of Joseph" (Amos 6:6)! They simply did not notice the signs of failure and destructiveness that were all around. In like manner, Isaiah can describe the "daughters of Zion" in terms of impervious self-indulgence:

> Because the daughters of Zion are haughty
> and walk with outstretched necks,
> glancing wantonly with their eyes,
> mincing along as they go,
> tinkling with their feet;
> the Lord will afflict with scabs the heads of
>   the daughters of Zion,
> and the Lord will lay bare their secret parts.
> (Isaiah 3:16–17)

And then, the prophet, in mocking understatement, provides an inventory of the tools of self-indulgence that will be forfeited:

> In that day the Lord will take away the finery
> of the anklets, the headbands, and the cres-
> cents; the pendants, the bracelets, and the
> scarfs; the headdresses, the armlets, the sashes,
> the perfume boxes, and the amulets; the
> signet rings and nose rings; the festal robes,
> the mantles, the cloaks, and the handbags;
> the garments of gauze, the linen garments, the
> turbans, and the veils. (vv. 18–23)

All the totems of privilege will be taken away! The city is
not a safe, happy, or beautiful venue for life or for faith!

Jeremiah, in his turn, can characterize the
predatory economy of the city wherein the poor are like
birds caught in a cage, where orphans and the needy
are disregarded:

> For scoundrels are found among my people;
> they take over the goods of others.
> Like fowlers they set a trap;
> they catch human beings.
> Like a cage full of birds,
> their houses are full of treachery;
> therefore they have become great and rich,
> they have grown fat and sleek.

> They know no limits in deeds of wickedness;
> they do not judge with justice the cause of the
>   orphan, to make it prosper,
> and they do not defend the rights of the
>   needy. (Jeremiah 5:26–28)

All of this is voiced concerning old Jerusalem. None of this, however, is noticed in the nostalgia of Psalm 137. The capacity for disregard of social reality suggests that the backward looking of the Psalm is on the lips of the elite who never experienced or noticed the socioeconomic realities of the city that were carefully kept from view. They had no notion of the underside of exploitation and oppression.

It is, at long last, 2 Isaiah who addresses such elite, exilic nostalgia. He utilizes an imperative that the privileged exiles should turn their attention away from their backward-tilted nostalgia to face forward into the new history that is now emerging:

> Do not remember the former things,
> or consider the things of old.
> I am about to do a new thing;
> now it springs forth, do you not perceive it?
>   (Isaiah 43:18–19)

It is time to relinquish that imagined past. It is time to notice that YHWH is making a new world before their eyes; and they are bid by God to accept and live into that future, even if it requires that they will not have such preeminence and influence in the newly emerging social scene. The exiles are urged to face up to the new reality.

As the tradition of Isaiah unfolds in its anticipated scenario, the poetry culminates in Isaiah 65:17–25 with a vision of a new heaven, a new earth, and a new Jerusalem. This new Jerusalem is not some heavenly escape. It is, rather, a viable city where society is marked in healthy ways:

- by *an absence of infant mortality*:

"No more shall there be in it an infant that
     lives but a few days,
or an old person who does not live out a
     lifetime;
for one who dies at a hundred years will be
     considered a youth,
and one who falls short of a hundred will be
     considered accursed" (Isaiah 65:20);

- by *a viable peaceable economy* absent of predatory threat:

"They shall build houses and inhabit them;
they shall plant vineyards and eat their fruit.
    They shall not build and another inhabit;
they shall not plant and another eat;
for like the days of a tree shall the days of my
        people be,
and my people shall long enjoy the work of
        their hands" (vv. 21–22);

- by *healthy child-bearing*, in which both mother and child are kept safe:

"They shall not labor in vain,
or bear children for calamity;
for they shall be offspring blessed by the Lord—
and their descendants as well" (v. 23);

- by *the acute attentiveness of God* to their prayers:

"Before they call I will answer,
while they are yet speaking I will hear" (v. 24); and

- by a full *reconciliation of all parts of the environment*:

"The wolf and the lamb shall feed together,
the lion shall eat straw like the ox;
but the serpent—its food shall be dust!
They shall not hurt or destroy on all my holy
    mountain,
says the Lord" (v. 25).

The prophetic point in 43:18–19 is a call away from escapist nostalgia to a new community, to be given in God's good governance that is marked by human life made possible, peaceable, and prosperous. We may conclude that covenantal-prophetic faith is exactly a refutation and rejection of the option of a "perfect, mythical yesteryear."

It is obvious that this same sequence of *nostalgia*, *summons to newness*, and *characterization of newness* readily pertains to our own sociopolitical crisis. The nostalgia of the right wing is to seek a return to the "good old days" of white male domination when everyone had their assigned roles to play, women were in their place, Blacks were subordinated, and gender roles were "unconfused." Clearly the revocation of *Roe* in *Dobbs v. Jackson* is a part of a return to the good old days that has been given loud and spectacular articulation by Donald Trump's MAGA. The America that he aims to make "great again" is one of white male domination. According to the inclination of the Supreme Court, the only Americans with explicit constitutional rights are white plantation owners. One can hear in such backward yearning for white male domination an echo of the Psalm:

> If I forget you, O Jerusalem,
> let my right hand wither!
> Let my tongue cling to the roof of my mouth,
> if I do not remember you,
> if I do not set Jerusalem above my highest joy.
>   (Psalm 137:5–6)

One need only substitute "white male domination" for "Jerusalem" and the point is clear enough. Such an arrangement of social power was indeed a "highest joy" for some. But for many, many others who do not appear in the blueprint of MAGA, the good old days were bad indeed. They were bad for women with such a low ceiling; they were bad for Blacks who were denied most opportunities; and they were bad for gays and lesbians who had to live covertly. Thus imagining a "perfect, mythical yesteryear" of white male domination is an exact counterpoint to an imagined joyous Jerusalem that conveniently skips over the truth-telling anguish of prophetic articulation.

The prophetic work, now as then, is to summon our body politic away from *nostalgia* for a world that never existed to engage social reality, and to receive the *newness that God promises us.* That emerging newness that we may take as a gift from God is indeed a multi-ethnic, multiracial society in which no one is granted special advantage, and in which no one is assigned to a subordinate role. That new future entrusted to us is a version of the old baptismal declaration:

Neither Jew nor Greek,
Neither slave nor free,
Neither male nor female. (Galatians 3:28)

That baptismal triad touches the continuing sore points among us concerning insider–outsider (that is, "clean and unclean") and economic equity between *genders*, *races*, and *social classes*. It is only those who live in a make-believe past who fear "replacement" from a world that never was. The new social arrangements coming upon us seek to exclude no one, but rather invite everyone to participate as a neighbor in a common enterprise of viable community.

The church, given its rootage in the memory of Jesus and its hope in the coming reign of God, is peculiarly situated to reiterate the summons of Isaiah 43:18–19. It is a call:

- to *stop the illusionary nostalgia*;
- to *notice the emerging newness* to be received as a gift from God, albeit an inconvenient gift, and;
- to *accept the work and responsibility* that goes with receiving life on new terms.

Those who are displaced from positions of power, privilege, and influence do not easily receive such news. So it is in the church as well. That is what sometimes causes the church to be resistant to change. But the God of the gospel is always making new. And we are always on the receiving end of God's newness. Our nostalgia will not stop the newness from God. It will only make the newness more painful for us. God's truth is indeed marching on. And we are at the work of catching up with that newness—receiving, embracing, and taking responsibility for that newness. God's truth is marching on, and all of our illusionary nostalgia will not stop that march toward justice, peace, and freedom by way of mercy and compassion.

3

Do Not Let the Doctor Leave You!*

The third claim is that **establishment experts are wrong, science is suspect.** This statement reflects the odd alliance between big business and less-educated people who (perhaps for good reason) harbor resentment against the "elites" who control a good deal of social power and the knowledge industry. The stake of big business is to refuse scientific data that leads to government intervention and regulation that impinges

---

* Because some readers will not have the text of Ben Sirach at hand, I have included the text itself at the end of this chapter.

25

upon profit. The stake of the "resenting class" is to insist that ordinary folk know what they need to know, and "expert knowledge" is a misrepresentation of the interests and "truth" of ordinary folk. And of course, the combination of greedy interests and resentment has been mobilized and harnessed by Donald Trump in the most effective ways, even when such a stance actually works against the interests of ordinary folk. Specifically, Trump has effectively made COVID-19 vaccinations into a political issue; to do so he had to insist that "medical science" is untrustworthy, so that his resentment-filled followers would be justified in defying and dismissing the claims of science. Thus a "know nothing" strategy has turned into a significant political movement wherein scientific learning is left suspect, and we are free to follow our interest and our passion without regard to what is known and established by science.

The church of course has a great stake in resisting such "know nothing" sentiment. It is not, however, so easy or obvious to appeal directly to Scripture on this issue, because the Bible was formulated in a prescientific age. The Bible places great accent on wisdom that is grounded in the reality and the rule of God.

> The fear of the Lord is the beginning of
>   knowledge;
> fools despise wisdom and instruction.
>   (Proverbs 1:7)

It is easy enough for anyone and everyone to claim to have *wisdom* without the claim making any appeal to *knowledge*.

In what follows I will pursue one suggestive connection between biblical claims and scientific knowledge. The case I consider is in Ben Sirach 38:1–15, a case I judge pertinent to us because it pertains to respect for medical science carried by doctors. Ben Sirach is a book in the Apocrypha of the Old Testament dated in the second century BCE, thus late in the Old Testament. Its lateness suggests that the writer, a scribe, lived and wrote at a time when Greek rationality was pressing upon covenantal faith, so that faith had to come to terms with the work of scientific knowledge. In this scribal text, one can see the intertwining of *faith* and *scientific knowledge*.

The writer is quite forthcoming concerning the claim made for the rule of God in the midst of scientific health care:

The Lord created them [doctors]. (v. 1)
The Lord created medicine out of the earth.
    (v. 4)
He gave skill to human beings. (v. 6)
From him health spreads over the earth. (v. 8)

The writer commends the practice of normal piety:

My child, when you are ill, do not delay,
but pray to the Lord, and he will heal you.
Give up your faults and direct your hands
    rightly,
and cleanse your heart from all sin.
Offer a sweet-smelling sacrifice, and a memo-
    rial portion of choice flour,
and pour oil on your offering, as much as you
    can afford. (vv. 9–11)

This is a quite traditional menu for the practice of traditional faith, with the affirmation that healing is in
God's good hands.

The counter theme of this text, however, is a commen-
dation of doctors, medical science, and medical practice:

Honor physicians for their services. (v. 1)
The skill of physicians makes them
distinguished,
and in the presence of the great they are
admired. (v. 3)

In addition to doctors, pharmacists are recognized as holy agents:

By them (marvelous works) the physician
heals and takes away pain;
the pharmacist makes a mixture from them. (v. 7)

And after the willing accommodation of traditional piety (prayer, confession, sacrifice), the writer continues:

Then [that is, after conventional piety has
been fully enacted],
Give the physician his place, for the Lord
created him;
Do not let him leave you, for you need him.
(v. 12)

The doctor has a legitimate, indispensable role to play in the healing process. The final line of verse 13 is quite insistent and noteworthy:

> Do not let him leave you, for you need him
> There may come a time when recovery lies in
>   the hands of the physicians. (vv. 12–13)

These lines imagine a doctor giving constant uninterrupted attention to the ill. This calls to mind for me a time when I was, in my high school days in a rural community, severely ill with pneumonia. I remember, even amid a high fever, that our family doctor, Dr. Koelling, drove twelve miles along country roads to call at our house every day. We waited each day for his arrival. We were reluctant to have him leave at the end of his call. Finally, as my illness continued, the doctor one day came with a new drug, "sulpha." (Thus even the pharmacist from Waverly, Missouri, got into the act.) This was before the discovery of penicillin. My family was deeply into faith and prayer, but we counted on the regular, reliable visits of the doctor, and did not want him to leave. In our faith, we counted heavily on his medical learning and his attentiveness. It must have been so for Ben Sirach, as he knew well about illness and healing. He knew about the importance of doctors and pharmacists. He had no reluctance about the reliability or urgency of scientific learning.

Finally his text reaches its conclusion with this affirmation:

> There may come a time when recovery lies in
>   the hands of physicians,
> for they too pray to the Lord
> that he grant them success in diagnosis and in
>   healing,
> for the sake of preserving life. (vv. 13–14)

The doctor is included in the sphere of faith! The doctor prays, even while the doctor practices the arts that belong to her science. Ben Sirach can discern no conflict between faith and piety and trust in good medical science. There need be no conflict because God created the doctors, God created medicine, and God presides over the best scientific practice of medicine.

In his commentary on this passage in *Wisdom in Israel*, Gerhard von Rad can observe, in his study of the wisdom tradition, that the term *kairos* (used as many as sixty times in Ben Sirach) denotes the right time for the moment of "discovery" (251). Among the remarkable discoveries that Ben Sirach notes is medical knowledge, just at the right time! Von Rad further observes that in general, the Old Testament affirms that healing belongs to God. It is God who heals and who is the healer (see Exodus 15:26). Because of this claim, medical science was not greatly developed:

As in the whole of the ancient Near East, medical science in Israel only succeeded very slowly in freeing itself from the strait-jacket of sacral ideas. But in Israel this process was also hampered by particular difficulties. It was expected to free itself not only from a deep-seated belief in demons or from taking renowned gods of healing into consideration (cf. 2 Kings 1:6), but also from what was a function and right of Yahweh's; for the idea that Yahweh alone could heal was represented in Israel in a particularly exclusive way (Exodus 15:26). And was not Yahweh also the one who caused illness? Was the latter perhaps a punishment? From this there arose the question whether one could prejudice Yahweh's privilege of healing. Here, in fact, the search for knowledge, otherwise active in a very impartial way, suddenly found itself with a problem which touched the very roots of faith in Yahweh. (135–36)

Because of this claim, questions had to be raised about medical science:

What was debatable was not the use of healing itself; the question, rather, was whether the practice of the art of medicine could be accorded a secular position which dispensed with sacral authorization. (136)

Thus the work was to establish *a zone of human possibility and human capacity* based on knowledge. Von Rad judges that our text in Ben Sirach is a "last, decisive step of the enlightenment" (136). By this "decisive step," the scriptural tradition establishes that *healing by YHWH* and *the practice of medical knowledge* constitute *a both/land* and not an *either/or*. That is the wise, informed settlement that faith reaches with knowledge in the confident affirmation that such human knowledge is exactly the gift of the creator God. That settlement, von Rad judges, was less than secure. He notices that verse 15, according to his translation, "threatens to nullify the carefully worked out process of legitimation" (136):

Whoever sins in the eyes of his Maker,
falls into the hands of the physician.

The matter is somewhat different in the rendering of the NRSV:

He who sins against his Maker
will be defiant toward the physician.

Either way, Ben Sirach made the case for the legitimacy of medical practice with a strong affirmation of the both/and of faith and science. In our own time and place, scientific knowledge concerning both global warming and viruses and vaccines need not be challenged by faith, because faith affirms that it is the creator God who has ordered the world in reliable ways that permit scientific learning.

In an early essay, "Job XXXVIII and Ancient Egyptian Wisdom," in *The Problem of the Hexateuch and Other Essays* (181–291), von Rad provides a study of "lists" of "cosmic and meteorological phenomena as well as of the animal kingdom" (285) that occur in Job 38 and Psalm 148. He concludes that these lists are part of a legacy of earlier Near Eastern learning, specifically from Egypt. I cite this study as evidence that scientific learning in the form of cataloging data was a long-term enterprise in the world of the Bible. When we consider that long-term enterprise, we may more fully appreciate the "last decisive step of the enlightenment" by Ben Sirach. The earlier evidence, as in Job 38, was still situated in a sacral sphere; but not so Ben Sirach.

Thus it follows, does it not, that the work of the church is to insist on the both/and of faith and scientific learning, and to make the case that good scientific learning is based in the broad, deep recognition of the ordered world willed and sustained by the creator God. From this it follows, further, that our best learning about global warming and our best learning about vaccines are to be seen as gifts made possible by the creator God, but then through the cumulative wisdom, insight, discipline, and imagination of research. The gain of "a secular position that dispensed with sacral authorization" is immense and our common life better for it. This gain needs to be valued and celebrated exactly on the grounds of faith.

The insistent refusal of the "community of resentment" is an attempt to roll back this "last decisive step" and to return our human destiny to the sacral sphere without reference to secular learning. A mantra of this attempted rollback is the recurring yard sign in our part of Michigan, "God's got this." I take this to voice an insistence that if we just trust God, we do not need scientific learning and must not be seduced or deceived by such learning. That politically motivated rollback, backed by dark money, is an abandonment of the hard-won understanding of both/and of faith and learning.

We might well pause amid our social crisis to celebrate the "both" of a *reliably ordered world* and the *shrewd discernments of science*. One side of the matter is readily sung by the church:

Oh Lord my God when I in awesome wonder
Consider all the worlds Thy hands have made
I see the stars, I hear the rolling thunder

Thy power throughout the universe displayed
Then sings my soul, my Savior God, to Thee
How great thou art, how great thou art
Then sings my soul, my Savior God, to Thee
How great thou art, how great Thou art.

The words attest the glorious grandeur of the creator. We might also add a verse to complete the "and" of both/and:

Then lifts my heart in glad appreciation,
For wisdom keen, as doctors soar,
That shows in welcome education,
Good medicine, healing galore.

This both/and of mature faith requires vigilance for the sake of our world and for the truth of God.

Ben Sirach 38:1–15:

Honor physicians for their services,
for the Lord created them;
for their gift of healing comes from the
    Most High,

and they are rewarded by the king.
The skill of physicians makes them
    distinguished,
and in the presence of the great they are
    admired.
The Lord created medicines out of the earth,
and the sensible will not despise them.
Was not water made sweet with a tree
in order that its power might be known?
And he gave skill to human beings
that he might be glorified in his marvelous
    works.
By them the physician heals and takes away
    pain;
the pharmacist makes a mixture from them.
God's works will not be finished;
and from him health spreads over all the
    earth.
My child, when you are ill, do not delay,
But pray to the Lord, and he will heal you.
Give up your faults and direct your hands
    rightly,
and cleanse your heart from all sin.

Offer sweet-smelling sacrifice, and a memorial
    portion of choice flour,
and pour oil on your offering, as much as you
    can afford.
Then give the physician his place, for the Lord
    created him;
Do not let him leave you, for you need him.
There may come a time when recovery lies in
    the hands of physicians,
for they too pray to the Lord
that he grant them success in diagnosis and in
    healing,
for the sake of preserving life.
He who sins against his Maker,
will be defiant toward the physician.

4

Public Truth amid Private Rumors

The fourth claim is that **we are entitled to our own facts.** This dismissal of reliable knowledge leads to unrestrained speculation. That in turn is readily open to conspiracy theories that do not need to be, or cannot be, fact-checked. Such an illusionary world, moreover, is fed by so-called *Fox News,* which sustains an alternative universe of illusionary imagination that feeds the most destructive political impulses among us.

Of course, the simplest, most direct, and most compelling refutation of this make-believe world of the

Right, featured so effectively by Donald Trump, is the terse response of Senator Daniel Patrick Moynihan:

> Everyone is entitled to his own opinion, but not to his own private facts.

The Right now regularly makes the claim of *alternative facts* when the *established facts* do not serve their political interest.

Obviously the church not only has a stake in resisting and refusing such right-wing claims but a deeper stake in the claim that truth and truthfulness are grounded in the reality of creation, that is itself grounded in the reliable "steadfast truth" of God's own life. The articulation of such truth grounded in lived reality is not always easy or obvious, as it depends upon a general consensus of norms for truth claims, and now even those norms are put in question.

It is not obvious to me what biblical text might offer a best response to the dismissal of science (and of reality), but I have been intrigued by the odd complex narrative of 2 Samuel 16:15–17:23. The big story in this text is that Absalom, son of David, is trying to seize the throne from his father. The narrative frames the action of Absalom as a "conspiracy":

> While Absalom was offering the sacrifices, he
> sent for Ahithophel the Gilonite, David's coun-
> selor, from his city Giloh. The *conspiracy* grew
> in strength, and the people with Absalom kept
> increasing. (2 Samuel 15:12)

This attempted usurpation ends for Absalom when
Joab, David's ever-ready hatchet man, and his men kill
Absalom (18:9–16). Short story: *rebellion mounted* and
rebellion defeated!

But in between the *initial insurrection* of Absalom
and *his defeat and death*, we have this complex narrative
of planning and negotiating the conduct of the conflict.
In that complex part of the narrative, the protagonists are
Ahithophel and Hushai, dubbed as intimates of David:

> Ahithophel was the *king's counselor*, and Hushai
> the Archite was the *king's friend*. (I Chronicles
> 27:33)

Already in this introduction to the two of them,
there is a distinction between them. Ahithophel is a
"counselor," but Hushai is his "friend," a more intimate
relationship. Both of them defect to the side of Absalom. While both were easily accepted into the camp

of Absalom, Hushai responds to the query of Absalom in quite ambiguous language, but he is accepted nonetheless (1 Samuel 16:15–19). Both of the royal advisers propose plans for Absalom's rebellion.

Ahithophel's plan, given in two parts, was well received. Ahithophel counseled Absalom first to commit a public gesture of seizure of the concubines of his royal father, thus acting the part of a king (16:21–23). Second, he proposes a quick strike of 12,000 soldiers to hit David while he is "weary and discouraged" (2 Samuel 17:1–4). His advice is reported by the narrator as "good counsel" (2 Samuel 16:23; 17:4), wise, concise, and likely to succeed.

Hushai, by contrast, turns out to be a double-dealer who covertly continues his loyalty to David. Thus Hushai offers a wholly unrealistic proposal to Absalom (2 Samuel 17:8–13). While Ahithophel has offered a limited, manageable military force readily mobilized, Hushai proposed, by contrast, the mobilization of the entire population "from Dan to Beersheba like the sand of the sea" (17:11), so that David can be hunted down wherever he hides. If David hides in a city, Hushai proposes that the entire city be dragged off into the valley by ropes until it is obliterated. Thus the pursuit of one man is by a scorched earth policy, quite a contrast to the plan of Ahithophel that had recognized that only one man was to be sought and killed. Beyond this quite bizarre plan, Hushai also warned David about how to hide and where to flee (2 Samuel 17:15–16).

Thus we are able to see that Hushai refused the expertise of David's military men and the long-running wisdom of practical steps. Instead, he proposed a set of alternative facts and alternative actions that had no connection to military or geographical reality. Hushai hoped that he could persuade Absalom, in his continuing loyalty to David, to disregard conventional expertise as a way to defeat Absalom.

Oddly enough, the point and counterpoint of Ahithophel and Hushai take place in a way that is disconnected from reality. The conduct of the rebellion and the defeat of Absalom take place apart from this oratorical contest between the two royal advisers. Hushai's plan is never seriously considered. And the plan of Ahithophel is foiled because of the covert action of Hushai, so David escaped from Absalom. Hushai, remaining loyal to David, comes out of the episode unscathed. By contrast, Ahithophel had bet on Absalom, and is disgraced. Consequently:

When Ahithophel saw that his counsel was not
followed, he saddled his donkey and went off
home to his own city. He set his house in order,
and hanged himself; he died and was buried in
the tomb of his father. (17:23)

We may identify two dimensions of this narrative that
do not appeal to the imaginative oration of these two
royal advisers. First, the actual defeat of Absalom was
accomplished otherwise, beyond the plan of either
piece of advice. **The fact is** (a fact that is beyond both
Ahithophel and Hushai) that Absalom was appre-
hended by Joab and killed by David's loyal general and
his men:

Joab said to the man who told him, "What,
you saw him! Why did you not strike him there
to the ground? I would have been glad to give
you ten pieces of silver and a belt." But the
man said to Joab, "Even if I felt in my hand the
weight of a thousand pieces of silver, I would
not raise my hand against the king's son; for
in our hearing the king commanded you and
Abishai and Ittai, saying: For my sake protect

the young man Absalom! On the other hand, if I had dealt treacherously against his life (and there is nothing hidden from the king), then you yourself would have stood aloof." Joab said, "I will not waste time like this with you." He took three spears in his hand, and thrust them into the heart of Absalom, while he was still alive in the oak. And ten young men, Joab's armor-bearers, surrounded Absalom and struck him, and killed him. (2 Samuel 18:11–15)

Joab did not need the myriad mobilization of Hushai; nor did he require the 12,000 proposed by Ahithophel. All he needed was his own "three spears," supported by his ten young men plus his long-running experience in such violent enterprises. Joab is unimpressed and unmoved by flamboyant rhetoric, and stays close to the ground in his ruthless military reasoning. He is indeed "an expert" in such matters as killing, an expertise for which Ahithophel and Hushai exhibit no respect. Joab knew what to do and how to do it, because he was experienced in the realities of war. His expertise would not be gainsaid by the rhetorical flights of the advisers.

But consider a second fact in the narrative. The narrator allows that there is an inexplicable "slippage" in the course of the narrative concerning the rejection of the good counsel of Ahithophel. David had anticipated that the deception of Hushai would defeat the counsel of Ahithophel (15:33–34). But David had also prayed,

O Lord, I pray you, turn the counsel of Ahithophel into foolishness. (15:31)

And then Ahithophel's advice was rejected, even as Hushai had urged (17:7). But the rejection is not explained by ordinary reasoning or by conventional common sense. The narrator is not reluctant to acknowledge another "fact" concerning the outcome of the narrative. He reports, laconically,

For the Lord had ordained to defeat the good counsel of Ahithophel, so that the Lord might bring ruin on Absalom. (17:14)

The verb "ordained" is a translation of the conventional word for "command." The Lord commanded the rejection of the advice of Ahithophel! Gerhard von Rad, in *The Problem of the Hexateuch and Other Essays* (198–201), has identified this text, along with 11:27 and 12:24, as texts that attest YHWH's decisive action in the narrative, even if that action is hidden from the actors in the narrative. Of the rejection of the "good counsel" of Ahithophel, von Rad writes:

> It is, then, at this point that David's fortunes change radically. Hushai's cunning advice was Absalom's undoing. We now understand why the historian should pause at this juncture, when the fate of Absalom is sealed, to point out to the reader the theological significance of the events. This was the turning-point in the rebellion, and the change in the situation was the work of God himself, who had heard the prayer of the King in his profound humiliation. (200)

In seeing God as the decisive actor in this narrative, von Rad concludes:

> Rather he [the narrator] depicts a succession of occurrences in which the chain of inherent

cause and effect is firmly knit up—so firmly indeed that the human eye discerns no point at which God could have put in his hand. Yet secretly it is he who has brought all to pass; all the threads are in his hands; his activity embraces the great political events no less than the hidden counsels of human hearts. All human affairs are the sphere of God's providential working. (201)

After we consider *the rhetorical contest of Ahithophel and Hushai*, *the realistic brutality of Joab*, and *the hidden effectiveness of YHWH*, we may return to the right-wing claim at the outset. The claim made here is for a bottom-up capacity for good knowledge. On the one hand, such a claim is a critique of any absolutism by elite experts. The experts must deal in probabilities, not certitudes. On the other hand, beyond the relativizing claim made by the right wing, there is a deep hidden purpose amid the human process, one we may call "providential," that is, God's capacity to "see beforehand." The right wing would make knowledge a contest between experts and conventional common sense. But that contest, convenient as it may be, is interrupted and relativized by the inscrutable holiness of God that is beyond both expertise and manipulation.

Given this remarkable claim made in the text, I reckon that it may be the church's best witness that the human process cannot be reduced to human capacity, human power, or human knowledge. There is another very different purpose at work among us. Faith is the bold, brave process by which we seek to align our own ideas and actions with that providential purpose. Witness to this long-running reality of the holy God of covenant is urgent work among us, urgent work that must be addressed. In the end, the prayer of the well-beloved David was answered (2 Samuel 15:31)!

An afterthought. If one finds this narrative too complex as an answer to the right-wing claim, then one might fall back on a simpler case concerning Jeremiah and Hananiah. After the first assault by Babylon on Jerusalem in 598 BCE, Hananiah opined that all would return to normal in two years:

> Thus says the Lord: This is how I will break the yoke of King Nebuchadnezzar of Babylon from the neck of all the nations within two years. (Jeremiah 28:11)

Hananiah lived in a wish world of royal imagination. He is immediately and brusquely countered by the prophet who sees the reality of the facts on the ground and declares:

> For thus says the Lord of hosts, the God of Israel: I have put an iron yoke on the neck of all the nations so that they may serve King Nebuchadnezzar of Babylon, and they shall indeed serve him; I have even given him the wild animals. (28:14)

We need have no doubt that Jeremiah would have resonated completely with the Yahwistic affirmation of 2 Samuel 17:14. There is indeed *another purpose* at work in the world that will not be mocked. Because of that purpose, the prophet can identify even the enemy, Nebuchadnezzar, as "servant of YHWH." God is indeed working out God's purpose. Neither right-wing fantasy nor absolutist elitism can escape the long, slow, hidden work of holiness that will, sooner or later, have its way.

> God is working His purpose out
> As year succeeds to year;

God is working his purpose out,
And the time is drawing near.
Nearer and nearer draws the time,
The time that shall surely be,
When the earth shall be filled with the glory
   of God
as the waters cover the sea.
All we can do is nothing worth
Unless God blesses the deed;
Vainly we hope for the harvest-tide
Till God gives life to the seed;
Yet near and nearer draws the time,
The time that shall surely be
When the earth shall be filled
with the glory of God
As the waters cover the sea. (*The Episcopal
   Hymnal* 412)

5

The Prophet on Profit

The fifth claim is that **short-term profits are everything.** It seems obvious enough that this claim is pernicious. The singular passionate pursuit of profit is destructive of serious honest human interaction, and serves to reduce other human beings to tradable, dispensable commodities.

The strategies for short-term profit are manifold and mostly obvious—high interest rates, manipulation of debt, low wages, corporate buyouts, and insistence on deregulation in order to permit exploitation. Such a singular pursuit of profit transforms the market from *a forum for commerce* into *a regulatory system* that marches to the tune of those who have the most leverage. The most extreme examples of such profit-seeking include corporate raiders like Carl Icahn and the way in which corporate managers like Jack Welch can game the system, on which see *The Man Who Broke the Market* by David Gelles. The cost of such greed is the destruction of the neighbor and the disappearance of the neighborhood, so that every would-be neighbor becomes either a competitor in the chase for money or a tool to be utilized for profit.

It is a truism that the covenantal-prophetic tradition of the Bible (as well as the sapiential tradition) advocates for the maintenance and sustenance of neighborliness in ways that limit and guard against the pursuit of profit. The church in general has too long been preoccupied with "spiritual matters" and "life-after-death" to give adequate attention to the matter of money as a potential for community well-being, as well as a threat to community well-being. I have been educated about the church's focus on money—or recognition of money as an issue for faith—by the remarkable study of the historian Peter Brown, *Through the Eye of the Needle: Wealth, the Fall of Rome, and the Making of Christianity in the West, 350–550 AD* (2012). Brown shows in plodding detail that the early church and its bishops were primarily preoccupied with delivering protective care to needy persons without resources. Such an accent contradicts our propensity to imagine that the early church and its bishops spent all of their time and energy articulating and refining the "Chalcedonian formula" concerning the Trinity. To the contrary, Brown chronicles the sustained effort of the bishops of the church to attend to the distribution and redistribution of much-needed economic resources.

But all of that changed, says Brown, in the fifth and sixth centuries when wealthy people began to participate in and then to dominate the church in its more established mode. With that changed population, energy shifted from *care for the poor* to the *self-preoccupation* of erecting extravagant mausoleums as tributes wealthy persons built for themselves. One by-product of this was that the priests of the church took on an other-worldly role, with haircuts to exhibit their other-worldly calling. Brown's book is enough to see that a dispute over money lies at the heart of issues concerning the nature, character, and mission of the church. And, of course, that dispute continues concerning the call of Christ's church to be fully and faithfully the "church of the poor." As a way into such critical thinking about the matter of money in the church, attention may be paid to *Eighth Century Prophets: A Social Analysis* (2003) by D. N. Premnath. His book focuses particularly on land accumulation and acquisition by wealthy people in the eighth century BCE, a process that caused the displacement of vulnerable people without social leverage. And the process of displacement of vulnerable people continues among us, on a large scale through colonialization.

There are many texts that might be a reference point for the refutation of this right-wing commitment to short-term profits. I have decided to consider, as a focal point of study, the poetic piece of Jeremiah 5:26–31. In this poetic utterance, the prophet Jeremiah follows a standard genre that includes an *indictment* for violation of Torah and an anticipated *sentence* as punishment for the violation.

The indictment the prophet issues concerns "scoundrels" (evil-doers):

> For scoundrels are found among my people;
> They take over the goods of others.
> Like fowlers they set a trap;
> they catch human beings.
> Like a cage full of birds,

their houses are full of treachery;
therefore they have become great and rich,
they have grown fat and sleek.
They know no limits in deeds of wickedness;
they do not judge with justice the cause of the
    orphan, to make it prosper,
and they do not defend the rights of the
    needy. (Jeremiah 5:26–29)

Verses 25–26a describe their predatory action whereby they "catch human beings." The charge lacks specificity, but the context indicates that they practice economic seizure in ways that reduce their victims (and targets of predation) to helplessness. The imagery suggests stealth and deception, practices that are ruthless, and policies that are covert. We can readily list the sorts of sharp dealing that were in play that reduced their targets to helplessness.

The result is the accumulation of great wealth. The poetry heaps up terms of negative characterization: *great/rich/fat/sleek*! These wealthy are so well off, with toned bodies that never toil or sweat, living off the work of others. That accumulation of ill-gotten wealth, moreover, has stark social consequences:

> They do not judge with justice the cause of
>   the orphan, to make it prosper,
> and they do not defend the rights of the
>   needy. (v. 28)

The poetry appeals to the standard carriers of economic vulnerability, "orphans and needy." From this pair we may infer the rest of the roster of the vulnerable, including "widows and immigrants," all of those without protective advocacy in a patriarchal system. The courts are rigged so that those sorts of people are without advocacy or protection, with no assured rights. The practice is an economy that is so tilted toward the powerful and the wealthy that there is no prospect or hope for any of the others. Such a characterization of the economy fits perfectly with the mantra "short-term profits." "Short-term" means no worry about or consideration of long-term social reality. No matter is beyond immediate satiation and self-indulgence, all made possible by the manipulation of economic policy and practice.

The "sentence" that follows the indictment in verse 29 is implied but not directly stated:

Shall I not punish these things? says the Lord,
and shall I not bring retribution on a nation
     such as this? (v. 29)

In disbelieving indignation, Jeremiah has God ask two questions:

Shall I not punish?
Shall I not bring retribution?

The questions are left unanswered by the poet. None-theless, we know the answer, because we know the ancient tradition and the track record of this Lord of emancipation. We have known the answer since the earlier moments of covenantal self-declaration. We have known the answer since the disclosure of Moses in the tradition of Deuteronomy:

You must not distort justice; you must not show
partiality; and you must not accept bribes, for
a bribe blinds the eyes of the wise and subverts
the cause of those who are in the right. Justice,
and only justice, you shall pursue, so that you

may live and occupy the land that the Lord your
God is giving you. (Deuteronomy 16:19–20)

That tradition, moreover, knows in preview the
same triad of the vulnerable to which justice
urgently pertains: widows, orphans, and immigrants
(Deuteronomy 10:18, 14:29, 16:11, 14, 24:17, 19,
26:12–13). Thus Jeremiah intends that Israel should
readily and intuitively know the answer to YHWH's
two questions:

> *Yes* . . . you shall punish those who seek
> short-term profit at the expense of the
> vulnerable;
> *Yes* . . . you shall take retribution on such a
> community of predators.

There is no uncertainty, according to the prophet,
because Israel lives in a world that is governed by the
Lord who attends exactly to the needs of the vulnerable. The self-serving "scoundrels" of usurpatious greed
are on a collision course with that nonnegotiable governance. It took the rest of the book of Jeremiah and a
few more years of history in Jerusalem for the answer

of punishment and retribution to become clear. But here the die is already cast for the city. The judgment of God against those who practice "unjust gain" generates certain unbearable consequences.

In our context it requires little imagination to see that the endless, unrestrained exercise of land and wealth accumulation in the pursuit of control, comfort, and security can only have negative outcomes. The poet knows, as does the entire prophetic tradition, that the divine response of punishment and retribution is not direct and super-spectacular. Rather, it is the slow grind of creation and history that works its retaliation on such a society in relentless ways.

Verses 30–31 appear to be a response to the foregoing that is perhaps uttered upon further reflection. The society addressed by the poet is now host to outcomes that are utterly shocking, outcomes one could never have imagined in the holy, blessed city. The most affrontive outcome imaginable is that the religious leadership should fail:

Prophets prophesy falsely,
Priests rule and preside over the treachery.

Finally, it comes down to religious leadership that has sold out and is nothing more than a cowardly echo of the dominant values of exploitation. Israel should indeed be shocked when its religious leaders are no longer capable of or willing to tell the hard truth rooted in the ancient tradition. So now among us, much of the religious community and its leadership have become a ready echo of uncaring distortion. And then the poet tells us why the religious leadership is so compromised:

My people love to have it so!

The prophet and priest simply respond to societal wishes and expectations. Such a sell-out puts the community in an impossible situation, so impossible that the poet in the last line wonders,

What will you do when the end comes? (v. 31)

The word translated "end" is "otherwise." What will you do when it is otherwise among you? What will you do when circumstances change dramatically? The poet sees that Israel and its religious leaders are ill-prepared for the big trouble that is to come. Israel has made no preparation and has given no thought to the coming trouble.

The matter is left unspecified. In the remainder of the book of Jeremiah, we learn that this unbearable otherwise to come is the onslaught of Babylon for which Israel is completely unprepared. In our time and place, this ominous sure-to-come "otherwise" is left without specification or articulation. It is easy enough to extrapolate that this coming "end" in our context ("Otherwise") is the environmental crisis. However that may be, it is self-evident that an economy passionately committed to short-term profit is quite unprepared for "otherwise." It is the bid of this poetry that the community turns its attention away from short-term profit, away from more individual self-sufficiency, away from the delivery of more consumer goods, away from the endless development of tools for control and comfort, in order to notice the reality of a world where the God who governs will not be mocked. In this demanding poetry, the "yes" of punishment and the "yes" of retribution are unremarkable. And now we are left to parse the poetry to see how it works on our lips, to see how it feels in our eyes, and to see how it may help us to a new inescapable attentiveness. In a monetized society like ancient Jerusalem (or in our own), the act of such poetic otherwise is urgent. Jeremiah hoped that even among the false-speaking prophets and ill-governing priests, there would be some faithful witnesses to "otherwise."

An addendum: Jesus is one of the heirs to the tradition of truth-telling. Concerning the practice of short-term profit, Jesus makes his stance clear in the most succinct way:

You cannot serve God and wealth. (Matthew 6:24)

In the Gospel of Luke, this same statement is a poetic conclusion after his parable of the cunning estate manager (Luke 16:13). This is a radical either/or. For the most part, most of us seek to have it both ways without choosing: God and money! The governing term is "serve." It is one thing to need money or to have money. It is a very different thing to "serve" money. That verbal usage suggests that the purpose of one's life is to exalt money, to hold it in honor, and so to organize one's life, one's effort, and one's imagination to do what it requires. The alternative here is a God whose long-term intent is the well-being of the vulnerable neighbors—widows, orphans, and immigrants. In the end it is an either/or. Jesus knew, as Jeremiah knew before him, that the future of the community consists of getting this either/or correct. The passion for short-term profit is based on a trouble-bringing choice. The wonder is that we already know the alternative. The work now is to mobilize the courage and sensibility to make the societal choice that must be made in order that the coming "otherwise" can be life-giving and not death-dealing. It is the pivot of this single, direct either/or that is the subject matter of the priests who govern well, and of the prophets who tell the truth.

In the wake of this stark either/or of Jesus, it is no wonder that the early church could host this truth in its epistolary corpus:

> For the love of money is a root of all kinds of evil, and in their eagerness to be rich some have wandered away from the faith and pierced themselves with many pains. (I Timothy 6:10)

It is not money that is the problem. It is the "love of money," a phrase that Jesus rendered as "serve money." In the antecedent verse, "Paul" writes of such greed:

> But those who want to be rich fall into temptation and are trapped by many senseless and harmful desires that plunge people into ruin and destruction. (v. 9)

Such "senseless and harmful desires" may plunge the entire community into "ruin and destruction." The good, hard, demanding news is that it can and must be otherwise. As Jeremiah knew in his time, we in our time know that our time is short indeed! It is no wonder that we have ringing in our ears the unanswered question of Jesus:

> For what will it profit them to gain the whole world and forfeit their life? (Mark 8:36; Matthew 6:21–28, Luke 9:21–27)

What indeed?!!!

6

A Sufficiency Other than Our Own

The sixth claim of the right wing is that **liberty equals selfishness**. This claim imagines, in a right-wing frame of reference, that "liberty" means to be totally unencumbered in the reach for wealth, control, and power. All of this, of course, is the extreme expression of the deep American creed of "individualism" at its most destructive. Andersen writes of this notion of liberty:

No gun control! No mandatory vaccinations!
No universal health insurance! So in the spring
of 2020, *of course* mobs of childish adults were

69

> excited to throw self-righteous tantrums on TV
> about being *grounded* by the mean grown-ups.
> While also playing soldier by carrying semiau-
> tomatic rifles in public. (370)

The inescapable outcome of such posturing is an unsafe society marked by an undercurrent of ready violence that preys upon the innocent and the vulnerable. Selfishness becomes the platform for ready violence, so that those who are smart enough, quick enough, ruthless enough, and lucky enough can imagine themselves to be self-sufficient. Such "self-sufficient" models, moreover, draw to themselves the admiration (not to say loyalty) of many wannabes who have no chance whatsoever to be self-sufficient, but who nonetheless are glad to be clothed in the mantle of "liberty."

It is easy enough to identify in Scripture examples of those who thought they could live in autonomous liberty. I could readily think of two such cases. In the first case, Pharaoh of Egypt is cited in the prophetic tradition as an example of imagined autonomy. I suppose there is a side glance at the claim of Egyptian religion wherein Pharaoh is a god. But it is more likely that the basis for such self-imagination is effective economic and military policy. For the prophet, the matter grows out of Israel's own Exodus tradition wherein Pharaoh is remembered as a violent, abusive exploiter who knows no limits in his ready exercise of coercion. In the prophetic oracle of Ezekiel 29:3–7 (extended into chapters 30–32), Pharaoh becomes the target of a prophetic assault and of divine diminishment. The prophetic charge against Pharaoh is that Pharaoh imagined and claimed that he himself had created the Nile River:

> I am against you,
> Pharaoh King of Egypt,
> the great dragon sprawling in the midst of its
> channels,
> saying, *"My Nile is my own;*
> I made it for myself."* (Ezekiel 29:3)

The claim is echoed in the prose verses that follow:

> Then you shall know that I am the lord. Because you said, *"The Nile is my own,* and I made it," therefore, I am against you, and against your channels, and I will make the land of Egypt

an utter waste and desolation, from Migdol to
Syene, as far as the border of Ethiopia. (Ezekiel
29:9–10)

The truth is exactly to the contrary, says the prophet.
It was the Nile that has "made" Pharaoh, that has produced his wealth and permitted his power. Thus Pharaoh, like many after him, has confused the creator
and the creation. And when the role of the creator goes
unacknowledged, it is easy enough to imagine that one
is self-made. Not only does Pharaoh imagine he is self-
made and that he himself created the Nile (the true
source of Egyptian life) but in the reprise of verses
9–10, YHWH reiterates the charge against him.

We know from an earlier poetic piece in Isaiah that
Assyria, a counterpoint to Egypt, had in the same way
imagined itself as the key actor, the subject of the powerful verbs:

With my many chariots
I have gone up the heights of the mountains,
to the far recesses of Lebanon;
I felled its tallest cedars,
its choicest cypresses;

I came to its remotest height,
its densest forest.
I dug wells and drank waters,
I dried up with the sole of my foot all the
    streams of Egypt. (Isaiah 37:24–26)

This is a generic boast of the powerful who readily imagine they are self-starters. Already in the oracle of Isaiah, the puffed-up "I" statements of would-be autonomy are countered by the "I" statement of YHWH, who, it is here claimed, will prevail.

Have you not heard that I determined it long
    ago?
I planned from days of old what now I bring
    to pass,
that you should make fortified cities crash into
    heaps of ruins . . .
I know your rising up and your sitting down,
your going out and coming in,
and your raging against me.
Because you have raged against me
and your arrogance has come to my ears,
I will put my hook in your nose

and my bit in your mouth;
I will turn you back on the way by which you
    came. (Isaiah 37:26, 28–29)

In the oracle of Ezekiel, the "I" of YHWH will prevail,
this time over Egypt:

I will put hooks in your jaws,
and make the fish of your channels stick to
    your scales.
I will draw you up from your channels,
with all the fish of your channels sticking to
    your scales.
I will fling you into the wilderness,
you and all the fish of your channels;
you shall fall in the open field,
and not be gathered and buried. (Ezekiel
    29:4–5)

The outcome of that countering divine "I" is the pri-
mary claim of the oracle:

Then all the inhabitants of Egypt shall know
that I am the Lord. (v. 5)

It is the hard lesson of the Exodus narrative, now belatedly reiterated, that YHWH is Lord, the lesson that brutality, with relentless insistence, has taught to Pharaoh (see Exodus 7:5, 17, 8:22, 11:7, 14:4). It was the same lesson for Assyria, and for every would-be autonomous agent. The much-acclaimed power of Pharaoh is decisively penultimate. In order to instruct Pharaoh in this reality, the Lord of history promises the utter devastation of the land of Egypt:

> No human foot shall pass through it, and no animal foot shall pass through it; it shall be uninhabited for forty years. I will make the land of Egypt a desolation among desolate countries; and her cities shall be a desolation forty years among cities that are laid waste. I will scatter the Egyptians among the nations, and disperse them among the countries. (Ezekiel 29:11–12)

And even in the belated divine resolve to "gather" the Egyptians who have been "scattered" by YHWH, the recovery of Egypt is modest and limited, never again to achieve its former power:

Further, thus says the Lord God: At the end of forty years I will gather the Egyptians from the peoples among whom they were scattered; and I will restore the fortunes of Egypt, and bring them back to the land of Pathros, the land of their origin; and there they shall be a lowly kingdom. It shall be the most lowly of the kingdoms, and never again exalt itself above the nations; and I will make them so small that they will never again rule over the nations. The Egyptians shall never again be the reliance of the house of Israel . . . Then *they shall know that I am the Lord God*. (Ezekiel 29:13–16)

The only good thing, in prophetic perspective, is that the Egyptians will know that YHWH is Lord! Of course this is all a poetic piece and nothing more. The poetry is preserved in Israel not because it is "true" but because it tells of *the ultimacy of YHWH* and *the penultimate status of every other claim*. The upshot is that autonomy is an illusion. Self-sufficiency is a mistaken pretense that will, in the end, yield to the will of the creator God. Pharaoh surely has great liberty of action. But finally his liberty reaches its limit and is curbed. It is curbed by the realities of history. Moreover, Israel's prophets insisted that the "realities of history" are the working out of divine will and divine purpose. And if Pharaoh would not learn that early, he would learn it late. Given this prophetic calculus, reference might be usefully made to *The Rise and Fall of the Great Powers: Economic Change and Military Conflict from 1500 to 2000*, by Paul Kennedy (1987). Kennedy surveys the course of the modern Spanish, Dutch, and British empires, and comes to the conclusion that in each case, economic prosperity ran amuck through excessive military spending. Those governments did not take into account the reality of limited resources and governed as though there were no limits. But, says Kennedy, the reality of limits could not be circumvented by the grand illusion of limitless resources. Kennedy never once mentions any theological claim in his analysis. It is easy to see how Israel's prophets would have taken up this recognition of "limits" and insist that it is the creator God who set such limits. Either way, liberty as selfishness could not work for Pharaoh or for any who came after him.

In a very different idiom, the parable of Jesus in Luke 12:13–21 takes up the same issue, only now the sphere of the narrative is not large-scale national ambition but (as usual with the parables of Jesus) an imagined individual managing his daily life. The framing of the parable is a warning against greed:

> Be on your guard against all kinds of greed; for one's life does not consist in the abundance of possessions. (Luke 12:15)

The parable concerns a rich man who produced abundance. This man is surely a model for self-sufficiency and self-aggrandizement. The man's produce outran his storage space. He considers what to do with his produce that he is unable to store. He might have thought to give some of it away. Or he might have considered cutting back on production in order to give his land rest for a season. But he did neither. Indeed, such options never occurred to him, because the former would have required him to recognize his needy neighbors. The latter would have required him to have respect for the land. But the farmer has no regard for his neighbors and no respect for the land. He is singularly preoccupied with his surplus that he intends to keep and protect. He makes plans for more storage (bigger barns!), so that he can keep it all for himself. His plan includes (not unlike Pharaoh; see Exodus 1:11 on the requirement of more storage capacity) a series of first-person verbs reflecting his assumed control of his future:

> I will do this;
>> I will pull down my barns;
>>> I will build bigger barns;
>>>> I will store all my grain and my goods.
>>>>> I will say to myself . . .

It is all "I" and "my," as it was for Pharaoh. There are no other characters in the story. We may imagine that his greedy wealth has isolated him. But he does not care, or even notice. He knew himself to be self-made and self-sufficient, so he never looked around for any other. He only addresses himself, "Soul." He issues imperatives to himself based on his isolation:

> Relax;
>> eat;
>>> drink;
>>>> be merry!

His is the predictable outcome of such a self-sufficient life in its success! But then, the parable jars:

"But God said to him!" (Luke 12:20)

Surely he was surprised by the abrupt address. Likely he believed in God, but it had never occurred to him that God would have anything to do with his agrarian prosperity. The preposition is an adversative. It interrupts a settled, peaceable narrative concerning a peaceable settled farm. It turns out that the man is not alone, as he had imagined. He had addressed himself as "Soul," but now he is called by a different name, "Fool." In that instant a "soul" has become a "fool" because he had misconstrued his true situation. It turns out that a *demand* is placed on him by the one who is a *commanding* presence: "Your life is being *demanded* of you." Now, for a second time, the term "rich" appears in the paragraph. He is "a rich man" (v. 16). But now "*not rich* toward God," *not rich* beyond himself, *not rich* toward the neighbors who are in the purview of this demanding God. His liberty-become-selfishness is shown to be a nonstarter, because this is a demand that is beyond his horizon.

In what follows in the sequence of the Lucan text, Jesus follows the parable with an instructive summons to his disciples, the ones who had signed on for his alternative life (Luke 12:22–34). He invites his disciples away from the endless vexations faced by the farmer in the parable, the same vexations that had before him beset Pharaoh. Such vexations concern food and clothing, and the stored "stuff" that preoccupies us, the stuff about which the birds and flowers seem not to know or care. Then Jesus commends his disciples to "your father." (Jesus has not yet arrived at rhetorical gender inclusiveness!) This "father" is the one who has curbed the grandeur of Pharaoh and who broke the spell of the rich farmer. This same father creator God knows what we need. This is "my father's world," and that world (still gendered in rhetoric) teems with care and provision that are assured for our common life.

Instead of worry and anxiety and storage and self-security, try the alternative governance! Give alms (v. 33). Serve a different purpose! Rely on different assurances! The parable is a potent articulation on its own. But its force is greatly enhanced by juxtaposition of the teaching in Luke 12:22–34. The parable, in this sequence, supplies an introduction to the teaching of

Jesus that is a summons to an alternative way in the world. The alternative way is alternative to greed that is propelled by anxiety. It is alternative to fear and violence. It is alternative to compulsive accumulation.

In our society that has run aground with fear, anxiety, greed, and eventually violence, this is an urgent moment for alternative. The good news is that we need not live by the pathologies of our society. Indeed, we cannot finally live the way of selfish greed, anxiety, and violence. We cannot, because as with Pharaoh, the creator will not tolerate such a way. We cannot live that way because, like the rich farmer, we are haunted by another holy address that rushes upon us occasionally. Those of us caught up in the cycle of fear, greed, and violence eventually are called by our right name, "Fool." And then we are addressed by the alternative.

What a way to think about the church! We church types are the people who know that liberty is not and cannot be selfishness, that accumulation does not work, that anxiety does no good, that greed never succeeds, and violence has no future. We know that. We are the people who affirm that. We do not always remember what we know, and we do not always live it out. But we meet together regularly to remind each other of what we know. What we know situates us differently in the world, yields a different set of hopes, and summons us to different duties. There is a relentless *communitarian* tilt to the gospel that refuses the mistaken American creed of "individualism." The good news is that we cannot and need not be self-sufficient.

7

Bread Shared
with All the Eaters

The seventh claim is that **inequality's not so bad.** This bold claim is not an expression of economic insight but only a shameless disclosure of the position of those who lead and fund the right wing. After all, I have never known anyone on the side of disadvantage who believes that inequality is a good thing. That sentiment can only be the advocacy of those who enjoy such shameless advantage. Of course, the right wing has been shrewd enough to recruit the support of many who will never arrive at their plus side of inequality. There is no reason to think that racism is not operative in this formulation. The great dread of the right wing is that Black persons should share advantage and be members of the plus side of inequality. The wide support of this position among those who are greatly disadvantaged, moreover, is likely because it is thinkable that at least Black persons suffer greater inequality, a fact that may make some inequality bearable. The entire claim is based on a sense of entitlement for those who benefit from excessive wealth, power, and control.

It requires no imagination at all to recognize that biblical faith, in gospel articulation, has no positive appreciation for inequality, but consistently insists that the wealthy and powerful are entitled to no special advantage. They are called to greater responsibility for the common good (Luke 12:48). Put in the most extreme form, the gospel anticipates a radical socioeconomic reversal, of last/first and first/last, and exalted/humbled and humbled/exalted.

As a consideration of the way in which the Bible refuses any positive appreciation for inequality, I propose that we linger over the manna narrative of Exodus 16. Back in Egypt, prior to the emancipatory wonder of the Exodus, we may believe that there was great inequality among Pharaoh and his entourage, the foremen, the taskmasters, and the slaves. Such a society was well ordered by rank and hierarchy. And as in every such ranked system, the rankings determined the goods and benefits apportioned unequally. The slaves could remember the "fleshpots" of Egypt wherein "we ate our fill of bread" (Exodus 16:3). But undoubtedly the food offered to slaves was very different from the food at the royal table. We can see the same reality in later Israel as the table of King Solomon was generously laden with ample meat (1 Kings 4:22–23), while the subsistence peasant farmers in Israel no doubt lived with sparse meat, if any. Thus, Pharaoh's regime was a model embodiment of inequality, unequal work, and no doubt unequal food, unequal drink, unequal rest, and unequal futures. One can imagine, in an anticipation of right-wing notions of inequality, one in Pharaoh's entourage exclaiming in the company of other members of the entourage, "Life is good." One could imagine a later Israelite engaged in the same self-congratulations, as scored by the prophet Amos:

> Alas for those who lie on beds of ivory,
> and lounge on their couches,
> and eat lamb from the flock,
> and calves from the stall;

> who sing idle songs to the sound of the harp,
> and like David improvise on instruments of
>   music;
> who drink wine from bowls,
> and anoint themselves with the finest oils . . .
>   (Amos 6:4–6)

And all the while the slave camps of Pharaoh enjoyed no such well-being. Instead,

> The Israelites groaned under their slavery and
> cried out. (Exodus 2:23)

Their groan set in motion a socioeconomic upheaval that upended Pharaoh's unequal practice of life and of bread.

Given this moment of emancipatory upheaval, our attention shifts (with the narrative) away from the ease of Pharaoh with his entourage to the void and anxiety of the wilderness where the escaped slaves found themselves. Here in the wilderness, there is no advantage, as the wilderness is a great leveler. Here there are no great storage units, no inequality. Everyone faced the same risks and felt the same dangers. The wilderness, it turned out, was a place of anxious equality.

In that venue of threat, there was shared anxiety with no social differentiations: "The whole congregation of Israelites complained" (Exodus 16:2). All of them! All were hungry! All were in need! All of them were nostalgic for the good old days of inequality and slavery. Surely they over-remembered:

If only we had died by the hand of the Lord
      in the land of Egypt,
when we sat by the fleshpots of Egypt and ate
      our fill of bread. (16:3)

The wonder of the narrative is that as soon as their desperate complaint is voiced in the wilderness, the response from the emancipatory God is prompt and promissory:

I am going to rain bread from heaven for you,
and each day the people shall go out and gather
enough for that day. (16:4)

Along with the prospect of *bread*—and subsequently of *meat* (quail; 16:12–13), and eventually *water* (17:1–7)—they also were promised that they would see "the glory of the Lord" (16:7). What a surprise that fit none of their expectations: *God's glory* in the *wilderness*! They had assumed that God's glory, along with pomp and circumstance, was all back in the land of Pharaoh. They had seen God's glory in connection with unequal splendor and wealth. But now they learned a radical new dimension of the God of the Exodus. It turns out that the natural habitat of God is not in Pharaoh's court but in the wilderness. It turns out that the wilderness is "occupied territory," not a waste and a void as it appeared to be. The "occupation" of the wilderness by the Lord of the Exodus means that the wilderness is a life-giving place. It is, however, a life-giving place barren of the social hierarchy of the kind they knew in Pharaoh's regime. Here there are no ranks, and so no ground for inequality. All could address the glory of God with urgent complaint. And all could receive the astonishing assurance by the Lord of the covenant: "I am going to rain bread from heaven on you" (16:4). Who knew? Who knew that the wilderness—void of Pharaoh's grain storage—could be a place for bread? The bread is promised; and the bread is given!

> When the layer of dew lifted, there on the surface of the wilderness was a fine flaky substance, as fine as frost on the ground. (16:14)

The narrator is at some pains to detail the bread. The careful phrase "fine flaky substance" tells us nothing. It is strange bread. It is bread unlike the bread of Pharaoh that is marked with sweat, and likely with blood, and certainly with inequality. But this new, different bread had none of those marks. And so they did not know. They did not know how to regard the bread that bore none of the marks of inequality. The explanation by Moses really tells them nothing about the bread, except that it is given by YHWH:

> Moses said to them, "It is the bread that the Lord has given you to eat." (16:15)

The bread comes with the command of the bread-giver who has presided over their emancipation:

> Gather as much of it as each of you needs, an omer to a person according to the number of persons, all providing for those in their own tents. (16:16)

The bread is assigned and received according to "need." (The Hebrew has, "In proportion to the eating of his mouth," that is, what each one needs to eat.) The focus is on *hunger* and the *satiation of hunger.*

The hungry Israelites in the wilderness promptly obeyed. They came to the bread with various hungers, and various appetites. But then, we get a most remarkable report on their consumption, one of the most remarkable verses in Scripture:

> The Israelites did so, some gathered more, some less. (16:17)

They did not all gather the same quantity of bread. Some had greater hunger; they gathered and ate more. Some were not as needy, and some gathered less and ate less. But there was no shortage, no lack. There was enough bread for everyone. We might not call that "equality." Or perhaps it is equality of appetite and satiation. But the point is otherwise. The report attests that YHWH, giver of strange bread peculiar to the wilderness, distributes differently and in measures commensurate to their need. No shortage; no need unmet!

It was "daily bread." It was bread wondrously given for the day. (Special provision is made for Sabbath day as an exception.) None of it is to be stored. None of it

is to be carried over to the next day. None of it is to be
made into a surplus. But then this:

But they did not listen. (16:20)

They did not listen to the qualification that the bread
was only for the day. They imagined that it could
be stored. Some set out to imitate the propensity of
Pharaoh to accumulate. If bread could be accumu-
lated, not only would there be more security but one
might have social leverage in the community. If some
could have more bread, they might be able to have their
say in the community, an exercise in leadership. They
might practice inequality. Thus even the bread of the
wilderness brings with it a compulsion to reiterate the
ways of Pharaoh. If one could store bread for an extra
day, or two extra days, and then three, one might begin
to see in the wilderness the erection of granaries for surplus. And then one would require a cheap labor force
to build the granaries, and so on clear to the return of
Pharaoh!

But the Lord of the wilderness will not have it so. The
Lord of emancipation intends that the covenant people
should need and receive the bread every day . . . for the

day. In order to enforce that lordly intent about the bread, we get *worms* in the bread, a *foul smell* of spoiled bread, and the *melting away* of the bread of fine flaky substance. This bread from heaven has a very short shelf life, because the bread-giver intends daily reliance on bread for the day. Wilderness life with YHWH is precarious, a day-to-day thing. Everything depends on the reliance of Israel on the bread given. Everything depends on the readiness to trust the bread-giver, and so to refuse the allure of a hoarded surplus is the route to inequality.

Israel's lyrical prayer life exults in the generous, reliable food supply given through the provisions of the creator:

> These all look to you to give them their food
>   in due season;
> when you give it to them, they gather it up;
> when you open your hand,
> they are filled with good things. (Psalm
>   104:27–28)

> The eyes of all look to you,
> and you give them *bread* for their food in due
>   season.

> You open your hand,
>   satisfying the desire of every living thing.
>   (Psalm 145:15–16)

That is why when we voice our table prayers, with hearts and heads lifted in wonder about food, we articulate our best creation theology. Every time we eat in gratitude, we remember how generous God is, and how deeply we depend on that daily gift. In celebration of the reliable presence of the creator, Isaiah can affirm:

> For as the rain and the snow come down from
>   heaven,
> and do not return there until they have
>   watered the earth,
> making it bring forth and sprout,
> giving seed to the sower and *bread to the eater*
>   . . . (Isaiah 55:10)

It is not bread for the predator. It is not bread for the powerful or the privileged. It is not bread for the lucky or the entitled. Rather, it is bread *for the eater*. It is bread given because all of God's creatures need to eat. The giver of bread is daily attentive.

We are left to imagine that Israel in the wilderness, from that awesome moment of "fine flaky substance," relied on the bread daily given from heaven. We may believe that such an arrangement, so characteristic of wilderness, pertained . . . until it did not. Eventually we are told of the end of that wilderness provision when Israel crossed over into the land of promise:

> The manna ceased on the day they ate the produce of the land, and the Israelites no longer had manna; they ate the crops of the land of Canaan that year. (Joshua 5:12)

What an awesome moment when Israel, so to say, "came of age" in the land of promise. Now, according to the tradition, Israel is plunged into Canaanite culture, Canaanite agriculture, and Canaanite religion, a plunge that constituted a defining crisis for Israel. With the new option of agriculture, it immediately became possible to store grain, to accumulate surplus, to gather social leverage, and so the practice of inequality. Without reliance on the daily gift of bread, Israel entered the world of production, distribution, and consumption, of leverage and surplus. (James C. Scott, in *Against the*

Grain: A Deep History of the Earliest States [2017], has detailed the way in which capacity for "grain storage" became a fierce tool of leverage and social control in the ancient world.)

Moses had anticipated this course of development in Israel:

> When you have eaten your fill and have built fine houses and live in them, and when your herds and flocks have multiplied, and your silver and gold is multiplied, and all that you have is multiplied, then do not exalt yourself, forgetting the Lord your God, who brought you out of the land of Egypt, out of the house of slavery, who led you through the great and terrible wilderness, an arid wasteland with poisonous snakes and scorpions. He made water flow for you from flint rock, and fed you in the wilderness with manna that your ancestors did not know, to humble you and to test you, and in the end to do you good. Do not say to yourself, "My power and the strength of my own hand have gotten me this wealth." (Deuteronomy 8:12–17)

Moses recognized that the land and its productive potential were seductive, and could lure Israel away from daily dependence and solidarity. Moses saw ahead of time that if Israel practiced amnesia about its past daily bread, it would imagine:

> My power and the strength of my own hand
> have gotten me this wealth. (v. 17)

Thus everything depends upon Israel's capacity and willingness to remember its rootage in the daily bread of the wilderness. In Judaism the remembrance of such bread is in the Passover meal. No doubt that is why the narrative in Joshua can speak of "the day after Passover" as Israel moved into the new economy:

> On the day after Passover, on that very day,
> they ate the produce of the land, unleavened
> cakes and parched grain. (Joshua 5:11)

The day after Passover, it is possible to be seduced, to forget the demanding equality of the wilderness, and to embrace the easy practice of inequality. In Christian tradition, it is the Eucharist that dramatizes our dependence on the bread that is given as the body of Christ. But, unfortunately, the Eucharist has been overlaid with so much misleading theology that one might not even suspect the link to manna generosity and manna dependence.

Thus Israel stands before *two modes of bread* and must decide. It always stands before this bread and must always decide again. There is the *bread of heaven* given daily that makes for community. And there is the *bread of production* that can be stored as surplus and distributed according to the whims of the powerful. The matter of these two kinds of bread, one that *practices equality of hunger* and one that *permits inequality* is, in my awareness, best exposited by Andrea Bieler and Luise Schottroff in *The Eucharist: Bodies, Bread, and Resurrection* (2007). They write of these options:

> The terrain of the *Homo oeconomicus* is the market exchange in which goods are exchanged for money. That exchange produces abstract relations between producers and consumers, relations not based on fulfillment of the basic needs of the individual or the community, but on the multiplication and accumulation

of money . . . The desire for more gives birth
to a craving for objects that move the *Homo
oeconomicus* away from the satisfaction of the
basic bodily needs of all people. His inner clock
ticks according to the news of the stock market.
He does not start with bodies or bread. He does
not take seriously the physical, psychological,
and spiritual needs of bodies as a prerequi-
site that is valid beyond the logic of economic
calculation. Men, women, and children are
considered human capital . . . The compulsion
to accumulate destroys rationality. (84, 89)

This matter is an urgent issue for the church,
because the choice of bread conditions a choice about
equality and inequality, about the shape of our future in
hope or fear, and about the power of *generosity or greed*.
It is clear that "inequality's not so bad" makes sense
only when bread can be reduced to a sterile, tradable
commodity. The biblical tradition, in both Jewish and
Christian usage, insists otherwise. It insists that bread
is a sign and practice of creaturely commonality among
us that refuses the social differentiations that legitimate
and enhance inequality.

The force and significance of this alternative bread lingers in the awareness of the apostle Paul. In his vigorous concern that the congregation in Corinth be generous in sharing with other congregations, Paul appeals to the old manna narrative. He bids the congregation to reflect on its abundance in order to be generous. In his appeal for such generosity, he writes:

As it is written,
    "The one who had much did not have too
       much,
    and the one who had little did not have too
       little." (2 Corinthians 8:15)

In a quote from the manna story, Paul bids the congregation to be generous according to the generosity of the creator God. With a bit of imagination, we may see that this narrative-based generosity concerns not only *church offerings* but also concerns *public policy* and taxation and the recognition that we all— the powerful and the vulnerable, the haves and the have-nots—depend upon the daily gift of bread, our granaries notwithstanding. It turns out that our excessive surpluses cause us to forget, and so to conclude that inequality is an acceptable social posture. It is not! The bread attests otherwise.

Finally, there is this little note about the obduracy to the disciples of Jesus. In the Gospel of Mark, Jesus had just provided bread for 5000 "men" (Mark 6:30–44). Soon after the disciples are said to be "afraid" (6:50), and then "utterly astonished." And then Mark adds laconically about their fear and their astonishment:

> They did not understand about the loaves, but their hearts were hardened. (Mark 6:52)

They misunderstood the bread! The reason they misunderstood is that they had "hard hearts," hearts not open to the generous assurances of God. When the bread is misunderstood, bad things happen. Bad things, like inequality, that soon begin to seem normal. Thus, we in the church must spend a great deal of energy in order to understand rightly about the bread, about the bread of heaven, the bread of Passover, the bread that is blessed and broken for us and for the world. To regard inequality as legitimate is a sure sign that the bread has been misunderstood.

8

Healing . . . without Money, without Price

The eighth claim is that **universal health care is tyranny.** This particular notion of "tyranny" is the simple recognition that good health-care policy requires taxation so that there can be adequate public funding to serve all the people in our nation concerning a most basic human need. This right-wing verdict reflects the deep dread that "somewhere someone undeserving will get something for nothing," even though the funders and shapers of the current right-wing movement have greatly benefited from public funds for a very long time. Even beyond that greedy fear, there is an implicit assumption that "lesser" people—those who do not effectively participate in the market—are undeserving and unimportant, or they do not, like the rest of us, in fact need or require good health care. There is, in this advocacy against the needy, a deeply shared, albeit tacit notion concerning social hierarchy, social solidarity, and social responsibility.

As an easy and obvious counter to such pernicious thinking, here I will focus on the remarkable narrative of 2 Kings 5. The chapter is among the narratives concerning Elisha, a larger-than-life figure who, for a time in the ninth century BCE, dominated the biblical narrative, and who offers in Israel a generative alternative to the failed and inept leadership of the royal dynasty in Northern Israel. At the outset we note that Elisha is completely uncredentialed. He has no notable background and no significant ancestors. Nonetheless, he has a reputation that must have been fostered by oral accounts of his inexplicable capacity to effect social transformations (see Walter Brueggemann, *Testimony to Otherwise* [2001]).

By the time we arrive at 2 Kings 5, Elisha has already enacted transformations that must have contributed to his reputation. He has provided oil for a hapless widow (2 Kings 4:1–7). He has raised from the dead the son of a wealthy woman (4–37). He has purified a large pot of stew (4:38–41). And he has fed a host of people with a modicum of food, with some left over (4:42–44). All of these narratives together constitute evidence that Elisha was gifted with an uncommon capacity for evoking well-being in a variety of difficult circumstances. His work is quite in contrast to the hapless unnamed king of Northern Israel, who exhibits no capacity to generate well-being for his realm.

Now in chapter 5, the drama opens in Syria, the long-running adversary of Israel. We may presume that the action is in Damascus, the capitol city of Syria. The opening scene concerns Naaman, a high-ranking military officer in Syria who was a mighty warrior with an important victory to his credit. (Our Israelite narrator rather puckishly credits his military victory to YHWH, this anticipating the claim to be made for YHWH subsequently in the narrative [v. 1; see v. 15].) For starters, Naaman is smitten with leprosy (v. 1). The disease is not only a threat to his health, but is an isolating disease because it was known to be immediately dangerous to the entire community, and so marked him as "unclean" in a way that required isolation. The general is about to lose his highly visible social standing! The narrative pivots on the welcome word of a young Israelite girl who was a war captive in Damascus. The young girl had, we know not how, heard of Elisha and his healing capacity (v. 3). Upon hearing the news of the general's infection, the girl tells what she knows of Elisha. Upon hearing of Elisha, Naaman receives permission from his king to travel to Israel to meet the king of Israel, and so to receive healing for his dread disease from his enemy. Kings have a way of caring for each other in spite of hostility, as in the recent case of protection and care for the shah of Iran.

The high-ranking general did not travel lightly to Israel. He carried with him and his entourage silver, gold, and many garments, all rich treasures that might make his overture for healing more acceptable in Israel. He anticipates that the wealth he brings with him will ease his welcome in hostile Samaria, the capitol city of Israel. He brings his *wealth* in order to secure his *health*! The king of Syria has anticipated that the king in Israel would assure the healing of the general, king-to-king! The nameless king of Israel, however, has no healing capacity, and regards the coming of the Syrian general into his city as at least an affront, if not a threat (v. 7). The king of Israel knows that only God can heal, and he himself possesses no God-given power to heal.

In contrast to the Israelite king who cannot heal, the next advance in the narrative is taken by Elisha, who heretofore had not been permitted into this narrative. Elisha is unabashed. He directs his king to send the general to him (v. 8). Elisha does not doubt his own capacity to heal the general and his leprosy. And so the general, surely bewildered by the default of the Israelite king, surely dismayed to be sent to this nobody, makes his way to Elisha's house (v. 9).

Elisha does not even get up out of his chair to welcome the general. He simply directs that the general should submit to an old Israelite practice of healing in the Jordan River. The general is now fully affronted; he expected a better welcome that would have honored his preeminence. He had anticipated better medical service than this. That, however, is all that is on offer from Elisha, nothing more than the modest Jordan River that was surely dwarfed by the great rivers of Syria well known by the general. It is as though the general is being dramatically reduced in stature and in prominence. Nonetheless the general is persuaded by his aides to submit to the simple requirement of the prophet. He follows the instruction he had been given. And healing happens!

> So he went down and immersed himself seven times in the Jordan, according to the word of the man of God; his flesh was restored like the flesh of a young boy, and he was clean. (2 Kings 5:14)

His diseased flesh was promptly clean and pure, as fresh as that of a baby! The narrator does not explain what happened, and exhibits no curiosity about it. We get only a matter-of-fact report that the prophet has effectively worked a healing for the general! Thus verse 14 is the conclusion of the narrative of healing.

But the narrative continues beyond the healing in a way that interests us for our topic. The general is exultant over his restored flesh:

> Now I know that there is no God in all the earth except in Israel; please accept a present from your servant. (v. 15)

He has been won over to the governance of YHWH, even at the expense of his own home-based gods. He utters the sweep of a doxology that only a new convert might utter. He takes his own healing as compelling evidence of YHWH's governance and capacity to restore. And then, as one does in a doctor's office, he offers to pay for his healing: "Please accept a present." The general knows the generic requirement: "Payment is due upon service." The general knows that medical care costs money. He is no cheapskate, but is both willing and able to pay whatever restoration may cost. "Spare no expense," the ready affirmation of people of means.

We have already seen a prophetic wonder in the healing. And now in verse 16 is a second prophetic wonder:

> As the Lord lives, whom I serve, I will accept nothing! He urged him to accept, but he refused. (v. 16)

Elisha's refusal of payment is part of his attestation that the healing is due to the wonder-working power of YHWH. He himself takes no credit, but gives full credit to the God who will take no payment. The narrative concerns the unambiguous delivery of free health care. The general makes one other request: to take back home with him some Israelite soil so that he, even at home, can properly worship the God of Israel, whom he confesses to be the only "God in all the earth." He allows to Elisha that his official duties as a "political general" will require him to participate in liturgies for the Syrian god, Rimmon, but he insists he will trust only YHWH; the rest is play-acting for the Syria public and for his king. Elisha has no quibble with the general's public requirements: "Go in peace" (v. 19).

The final paragraph of the narrative, verses 20–27, exhibit the way in which health care is ambiguously connected to money. The servant of Elisha, Gehazi, is quick to grasp the opportunity for exploitation. But his effort to exploit health care for gain does not go well. His greed promptly runs afoul of the will of God for free health care and of the intent of the prophet. Gehazi ends, in the puckishness of the narrative, as the new carrier of leprosy of which the general had been healed. While both Gehazi, the servant boy, and Naaman, the Syrian general, assume health care is linked to money,

Elisha insists otherwise. He is a champion of free health care!

Now I am quick to recognize that it is a very long stretch from this ancient narrative of Elisha to our current health care crisis. The narrative nonetheless is enough to suggest that we can easily trace out *two practices of health care*, just as we have heretofore seen *two practices of bread (food)*. We have previously seen that there is the "bread of heaven" freely given, bread for all of God's creatures, and bread wrought through market forces. *Mutatis mutandis*, we can readily see that there are two notions of health-care delivery: one is the free offer of transformative care; the other is a calculating market-driven health care that is propelled by *Homo oeconomicus* and is designed for profit. Gehazi and Naaman together are prepared to participate in the latter, and assume that it is normal practice to be accepted. But Elisha is a carrier of and advocate for the former, that is, free health care.

It is some distance from Elisha's free gift of health care to publicly financed health care among us, or as it is polemically termed, "socialized medicine." Those who easily benefit from monetized health care are readily able to call a free offer of such care as "tyranny." But to all others, such free health care, publicly financed, is simply the practice of the community caring for its own, and mobilizing its common resources for that care for all.

The trajectory of healing from Elisha extends, in Christian tradition, to the health-care ministry of Jesus. Indeed, Jesus may be seen in a stylized way, as a reiterating of the ministry of Elisha with the same readiness for good health care that is not monetized. The gospel narrative is saturated with testimony that Jesus was a healer among the common people. His reach was indeed "universal" without monetization, and none thought his work to be tyrannical:

> So his fame spread throughout all Syria, and they brought to him all the sick, those who were afflicted with various diseases and pains, demoniacs, epileptics, and paralytics, and he cured them. (Matthew 4:24)
>
> Then Jesus went about all the cities and villages, teaching in their synagogues, and proclaiming the good news of the kingdom, and curing every disease and every sickness. (9:35)

> Great crowds came to him, bringing with
> them the lame, the maimed, the blind, the
> mute, and many others. They put them at his
> feet, and he cured them, so that the crowd
> was amazed when they saw the mute speak-
> ing, the maimed whole, the lame walking, and
> the blind seeing. And they praised the God of
> Israel. (Matthew 15:30–31; see also 8:7–13,
> 12:15, 22, 14:14, 19:2, 21:14)

We may recognize that the dispute that Jesus faced concerning healing on the Sabbath is disputed between *two practices of health care*, the one that is universal and free, the other that is controlled, managed, super-vised, and regulated to advance the interests of the social leaders (Matthew 12:9–14). Just above, I wrote, "None thought his work to be tyrannical." But that is not correct. The leadership surely thought that his health care was oppressive, because it disputed the monetary control they were able to exercise in health-care practice. He had sent forth healing forces into the world that they found impossible to regulate or monetize. His readiness for transformative health care was unencumbered by their regulations.

Beyond that, we may also notice that Jesus extends his health-care capacity to the work of his disciples as well. His disciples were to do the work of healing:

> Then Jesus summoned his twelve disciples and gave them authority over unclean spirits, to cast them out, and to cure every disease and every sickness . . . Cure the sick, raise the dead, cleanse lepers, cast out demons. You received without payment; give without payment. (Matthew 10:1, 8)

In verse 8 it is to be especially noted that much healing work is "without payment," thus an echo of the refusal of payment by Elisha. The narrative of Matthew, moreover, is honest to recognize that the capacity of the disciples to heal was limited by the measure of their faith, and their trust in the restorative powers of God:

> When they came to the crowd, a man came to him, knelt before him, and said, "Lord, have mercy on my son, for he is an epileptic and he suffers terribly; he often falls into the fire and

often into the water. And I brought him to
your disciples, but they could not cure him."
Jesus answered, "You faithless and perverse
generation, how much longer must I be with
you? How much longer must I put up with
you? Bring him here to me." And Jesus rebuked
the demon, and it came out of him, and the
boy was cured instantly. (Matthew 17:14–18)

It was the "little faith" of the disciples that is central to
the episode.

In the narrative of the book of Acts, the healing
work of the church is duly noted. Most spectacular is
the healing of the blind beggar by Peter and John:

But Peter said, "I have no silver or gold, but
what I have I give you; in the name of Jesus
Christ of Nazareth, stand up and walk." And
he took him by the right hand and raised
him up; and immediately his feet and ankles
were made strong. Jumping up, he stood and
began to walk, and entered the temple with
them, walking and leaping and praising God.
(Acts 3:6–7)

Indeed, it is reported that the man is given "perfect health" (3:16). This transformative act led to the arrest and imprisonment of the apostles. It is clear that the establishment is made nervous by the offer of free healing. That healing work of the apostles is nonetheless otherwise attested in the book of Acts:

> A great number of people would also gather from the towns around Jerusalem, bringing the sick and those tormented by unclean spirits, and they were all cured. (Acts 5:16)
>
> The crowds with one accord listened eagerly to what was said by Philip, hearing and seeing the signs that he did, for unclean spirits, crying with loud shrieks, came out of many who were possessed; and many others who were paralyzed or lame were cured. So there was great joy in the city. (Acts 8:6–8)
>
> It so happened that the father of Publius lay sick in bed with fever and dysentery. Paul visited him and cured him by praying and putting his hands on him. After this happened, the rest of the people on the island who had diseases also came and were cured. (Acts 28:8–9)

The church believes and trusts that God's restorative power is at work in the world. It attests, moreover, that that restorative power was singularly concentrated in the person and life of Jesus. The church does not doubt that, beyond that, this same capacity and responsibility for restoration is its continuing work. It is for this reason that the church has steadfastly been committed to "medical missionaries," and has long been invested in health-care practice and delivery through hospitals and health care. As on every other front, the church resists the monetization of the delivery of basic services in meeting basic human needs, because monetization of such services as healing can and surely will lead to ranked service. Such service is predictably better for the well-off than for the poor and disadvantaged. Our current monetized health-care system is yet another instance of "separate but equal" in which we have long since known that "separate" for the moneyed and for the poor is not and cannot be "equal." It is unequal not only in expenditure but in care, attentiveness, and in commitment to heal. It is time for the church to make a vigorous case that it is not "universal health care" that is "tyrannical." It is exactly the opposite: monetized health care is tyrannical and ill serves the common good. The church, along with the synagogue, can gladly affirm:

> Bless the Lord . . .
> who forgives all your iniquity,
> who *heals all your diseases*,
> who redeems your life from the Pit,
> who crowns you with steadfast love and
>   mercy,
> who satisfies you with good as long as you
>   live . . . (Psalm 103:3–5)

This doxology is a catalog of God's recurring acts of transformation of the world. But of course the church, as well as the synagogue, knows that *God's transformative work* is at the same time *human transformative work*. It is faithful human responsibility to be about the task, as the psalm says, of forgiveness, healing, redemption, crowning, and satisfying. It is a wonder (as well as a fact) that free healing is *the human performance of God's work*. Elisha knew that. So did Jesus! So does the church and the synagogue. Indeed, the only ones who do not know this are the ones who have a monetary stake in doing health care otherwise. In the second "woe oracle" of the "woes" of Matthew 23, it goes this way:

> But woe to you, scribes and Pharisees, hypocrites! For you lock people out of the kingdom of heaven. (Matthew 23:13)

The regulatory authorities serve those who benefit from control, who "lock out" people from the kingdom of heaven, that is, from the common good of the community. (The same phrase, "lock out," is used in I John 3:17 with a question pertinent to our topic: "How does God's love abide in anyone who has the world's goods and sees a brother or sister in need and yet *refuses* help?") Monetization is an effective mode of "lock out." Such norms and requirements keep the disadvantaged from adequate participation in the blessings of the common good. A monetized health-care system is an effective "lock out." Those who do so are yet again and always addressed by the "woe" of the Lord of well-being who intends that none should be "locked out" of the basic resources for life and well-being.

Evil Geniuses: A Reprise

In the previous eight chapters, I have been engaged in response to the remarkable, important book of Kurt Andersen, *Evil Geniuses: The Unmaking of America: A Recent History* (2020). In the book Andersen traces the long-range planning of the right wing to take over the government, a plan that has well-nigh succeeded! Near the end of his book (368–70), Andersen lists eight elements of the playbook of the right wing that have evoked support and guided action:

1. Government is bad.
2. Belief in our perfect, mythical yesteryear.
3. Establishment experts are wrong, science is suspect.

4. Entitled to our own facts.
5. Short-term profits are everything.
6. Liberty equals selfishness.
7. Inequality's not so bad.
8. Universal health care is tyranny.

In my responsive expositions, I have engaged each of these claims, and have sought to show how and why and in what way gospel faith, rooted in the Bible, refuses these claims and takes them to be false. I have entitled my eight responses in this way:

1. The Possibility of Good Governance.
2. The Discomfiting Gift of Newness.
3. Do Not Let the Doctor Leave You!
4. Public Truth amid Private Rumors.
5. The Prophet on Profit.
6. A Sufficiency Other than Our Own.
7. Bread Shared by All the Eaters.
8. Healing . . . without Money, without Price.

In these discussions I have proposed exact counters to the misguided and distorted expression of the way forward by the right wing. I suggest that this sketch of an alternative way of thinking about our public life in sum refuses and contradicts the claims of the right wing.

1. Good government is possible. All that is required are brave, publicly oriented citizens who care enough about the common good to restrain any greedy extortion for personal gain or advantage. It is ludicrous to propose that our public institutions, grounded in the Constitution and rooted in democratic political theory, cannot provide us with such leadership. The case for the public good is at the heart biblical faith, most notably when the book of Deuteronomy, with its offer of separated powers of government, can be taken as an early radical model of constitutional government, a model, moreover, championed by Israel's prophetic tradition (see S. Dean McBride, "Polity of the Covenant People: The Book of Deuteronomy," *Interpretation* 41 (1987): 229–44).

2. Biblical faith in sum compellingly resists and refuses nostalgia for any "good old days" (see Isaiah 43:18–19). It affirms, characteristically, that our eye should be on an emerging public future, on the work of the God of the gospel, exactly the creation of new life—new wine to be contained in new wine skins! To linger with a wish for the return of the good old days is then a refusal of this future-generating God and the

future that God intends. Our current nostalgia, moreover, is specifically for a return to the good old days of
white male control and privilege. It turns out that is
what the current phrase "great again" intends. It is a
futile hope to contradict the promissory energy of the
God of the gospel, and the emergence of a new, viable,
neighborly public future.

3. The dismissal of science is a dismissal of the
God-given human capacity and human responsibility
to live knowingly in God's world. We have long since
understood that responsible faith and responsible science have no need for contradiction. Our best knowing
is an act of faith and trust in the ordered world willed
by the creator. The wisdom tradition of Israel embraces
both the continuing mystery of God's world and the
human capacity to do the work of understanding and
interpretation. It is not an either/or:

It is the glory of God to conceal things,
but the glory of kings to search things out.
(Proverbs 25:2)

It is the proper business of the church to support good
scientific work as a way to receive and exult in both

the wondrous gift of life and the wondrous vocation of human agency for the maintenance and enhancement of God-given life.

4. We may take as paradigmatic for the claim of truth the dramatic moment when the Roman governor who stood in wonderment before Jesus asked, "What is truth?" (John 18:38). Of this confrontation, Paul Lehmann, in *The Transfiguration of Politics: The Presence and Power of Jesus of Nazareth in and over Human Affairs* (1975, 55), can write:

> The question of the establishment is up; the question whose world is this, and by what or whose authority . . . Pilate's honest perplexity about truth was revealed in his puzzlement that power should require truth if it sought to command authority. Pilate was a realist whose chain-of-command conception of power made it impossible for him to understand the lifestyle of Jesus. Confronted by the lifestyle of Jesus, however, the worldly realism of Pilate is exposed as pseudo-realism . . . Jesus, on the other hand, affirms, both by conviction and by role, that the only authority power has is the authority of truth.

In his bewilderment the Roman governor discovered that his grasp on power and authority is illusionary, because he is unable to outflank or outwit the reliable governance of the creator God, who stands before him in human embodiment. The governor discovers that power is not given over to clever management or cunning ideology but is woven into the fabric of a life of self-giving vulnerable generosity. No amount of political posturing or epistemological flim-flam will alter that governance that we have most unambiguously witnessed in Jesus of Nazareth.

5. It is clear that economic practice that is solely committed to private gain and individual advancement is an enterprise that can only result in a deathly jungle of greed, fear, and violence. It is impossible to pursue profit in a selfish way without disrupting and damaging the political and social infrastructure upon which the life of all of us depends. Such a pursuit of personal profit is an unsustainable illusion, because it imagines that it can succeed without reliance on the gifts of the social, economic, and political order. It is an illusion because our lives depend upon attention to, investment in, and commitment to the common good. The Bible is unflinching and unaccommodating in its insistence upon the priority of the community upon which the

life of the individual depends. It is for that reason that the great mantras of prophetic faith endlessly insist upon *justice, righteousness, compassion, steadfast love,* and *faithfulness.* No amount of private gain or private property will substitute for that, nor will it provide, of itself, the requirements of a sustainable political economy.

6. Self-sufficiency is of course an illusion. There are no self-made or self-sufficient persons. Thus, the church can innocently sing:

> Now thank we all our God with heart and
>   hands and voices,
> who wondrous things hath done, in whom
>   this world rejoices;
> who, from our mothers' arms hath blessed us
>   on our way
> with countless gifts of love, and still is ours
>   today.
> ("Now Thank We All Our God," *Glory to God:*
> *Hymns, Psalms & Spiritual Songs,* 643)

The stanza of the hymn nicely affirms both the life-giving reality of our mothers and the abiding sustenance of God. Both are required for a viable life. As innocent as these lines in the hymn are, they nonetheless convey the truth of our lives. From our births—even before our births!—we have each been blessed; the blessing of God, moreover, has unfailingly taken human form; a host of persons in their constant attentiveness have surely "blessed us on our way." We, every one of us, are on the receiving end of life long before we become agents or guarantors of our own life or of the well-being of our community. The great fear of capitalist ideology is the notion that we may be on the receiving end of the processes of life. That is why capitalism, at its most unrestrained, seeks to abolish Sabbath rest, because Sabbath is an acknowledgment that what we have and what we are constitutes a gift that sustains our lives. Such a false notion as self-sufficiency contradicts the facts of our lives. The plain truth is that our lives are a gift, and we are dependent upon a host of givers. The only appropriate response to this recognition is gratitude that makes for generosity. That is why we are endlessly haunted by the question of the apostle:

> What do you have that you did not receive? And if you received it, why do you boast as if it were not a gift? (1 Corinthians 4:7)

The answer to the first question of course is "nothing." I have nothing that I did not receive!

7. It may be that some measure of inequality is inescapable in a complex economy. It is, however, quite another matter to advocate that inequality is a social practice that is to be valued, endorsed, and sought after. The Bible is preoccupied—long before Karl Marx—with the problem of haves and have-nots, of the legitimate claims of the have-nots, and the dangers of the haves who possess in excess. While some inequality is not only inescapable but bearable, the extremes of inequality featuring greed in policy and in practice are irresponsible and cannot end well for our society. The apostle has written that "greed is idolatry" (Colossians 3:5). That is, unbridled self-serving is the actual practice of an alien god. In the Old Testament, the name of that greedy, endlessly consuming god is Baal. But the name does not matter. In the end greed is a practice that can only lead to a false life, and to the failure and defeat of truthfulness, justice, and social well-being. The God of the gospel issues an endless summons to us to live in a generous, generative mode that has all kinds of important implications for policy, as well as for practice. The Torah and the prophets are filled

with summons for "justice," for the creation and maintenance of dignity, security, and well-being for every
member of the community. In the coming Kingdom of
God, there are no throw-away persons. There are only
neighbors who have yet to be admitted to the table of
abundance.

8. I have laid out a case for universal health care.
Healing is not a private property. It is a practice that
participates in the generous promises of the creator
as human agents work for a common well-being. To
imagine that support for those life resources should be
doled out according to money is a ludicrous mockery
of the way of the creator. Indeed, the wisdom tradition has well seen that the dismissal of care for a needy
neighbor is an affront to the reality of God:

Those who mock the poor insult their Maker;
those who are glad at calamity will not go
unpunished. (Proverbs 17:4)

Our shared failure concerning health care in our society is indeed a blasphemy against the God who will
not be mocked, and who eventually will not abide the
mockery of any of God's own well-beloved creatures.

While I have dwelt on these eight points and made specific responses to these eight claims of the right wing as articulated by Andersen, I take the import of my responses to be cumulative. That is, my eight responses are not distinct matters. They are, rather, all of a piece of a single claim concerning the will of the creator for the well-being of creation. I intend that the cumulative effect of these pieces may be grounding for the awareness of the quite distinctive claim the gospel makes upon our common life.

There is little to be gained in making arguments against these right-wing claims. It is far better, in my judgment, to use our energy to see that the sum of these points provide grounding for an alternative witness and an alternative practice by the church. Because of our long-running cultural accommodation of the church, many in the church do not fully realize how radically alternative are the claims of the gospel. In our current circumstance of rising fascism and the jeopardy of our democratic institutions, it is time for the church to be awakened for its articulation and practice of alternative. Thus, I hope that these expositions may provide ground for the church and its pastors to be about the business of alternative identity and witness in the world. We are deeply at odds with the right-wing distortions named here, in a struggle with uncritical nationalism, with the rise of white racism and anti-Semitism. The distorted claims of the right wing provide an opportunity for such work, in which the church can make a difference in the maintenance of our democratic institutions and our democratic ways of life that honors every member of our political community. The maintenance of that common life relies upon faithful, bold, and courageous leadership, not least among pastors.